LIVE MORE

MORE

Happy

SCIENTIFICALLY PROVEN WAYS
TO LIFT YOUR MOOD AND YOUR LIFE

Dr Darren Morton

Disclaimer: The ideas, concepts and opinions expressed in this work are intended to be used for educational purposes only. This work is sold and distributed with the understanding that the authors and publisher are not rendering medical advice of any kind, nor is this work intended to (a) replace competent and licensed professional medical advice from a physician to a patient, or (b) diagnose, prescribe or treat any disease, condition, illness or injury. Readers should seek the advice of their individual doctor or other health-care provider prior to and during participation in these lifestyle activities. The author and publisher of this work disclaim any and all responsibility to any person or entity for any liability, loss or damage caused or alleged to be caused directly or indirectly as a result of the use, application or interpretation of the material in this work.

For more information or to purchase additional copies of this book, visit **www.DrDarrenMorton.com**

SIGNS
PUBLISHING®
Established 1885

Proudly published and printed in Australia by
Signs Publishing
Warburton, Victoria.

This book was
Edited by Nathan Brown
Proofread by Lindy Schneider
Cover design by Shane Winfield
Internal images design by Jared Madden

Typeset in Berkeley Book 12.25/17

ISBN (print edition) 978 1 925044 72 0
ISBN (ebook edition) 978 1 925044 73 7

Dedicated to

Sarah, Olivia, Elijah and Caleb
for making me happy.

Contents

Introduction

I want you to be happier and I am certain that this book can help you achieve it.

In 2006, I wrote a book titled *Seven Secrets for Feeling Fantastic* in which I described in simple terms how the part of our brain responsible for how we feel—our emotions—is wired and how we can put it in a better state so we can feel better, more often. As the title indicated, it had a positive spin. I intentionally wrote the book not so much for people who were clinically depressed, but for those who just wanted to be more "up" than they were.

What truly—and pleasantly—surprised me was the feedback I received in response to the book. It resonated with readers, and I received many reports from individuals who told me how it had lifted them and helped them live more. Some of the stories were incredibly encouraging. But what I wasn't prepared for were the uplifting stories from people who were desperately "down" but were able to come back to life through the strategies I had shared in the book.

I discovered that the strategies for boosting emotional wellbeing and becoming happier, which I present again in this book, lift people regardless of how high or low they are on the emotional ladder. My research has now shown that, on average, people who put the content of this book into practice experience a 30 per cent reduction in depressive symptoms, anxiety and stress, and a 20 per cent improvement in their mental health and vitality.[1]

And this includes men! Some men seem to be turned off by the topic of "feelings", but we men have feelings too—for example, we feel hungry! Seriously, men and women, young and old, all desire to be emotionally up, so this book is for you—whoever you are.

Live More Happy builds on my first book *Seven Secrets for Feeling Fantastic* and draws together the latest discoveries from neuroscience, positive psychology and lifestyle medicine—three areas of study, research and healthcare that have exploded during the past decade.

I am incredibly passionate about sharing the messages in this book. Everyone needs to know them because feeling down is on the up. In Australia, which is rated among the top 10 "happiest" countries in the world,[2] antidepressant usage has doubled in the past decade, making them the most commonly used medications, taken by approximately one in 10 adults every day.[3] The statistics are even more concerning in countries such as the United States.[4] Studies show that only about 20 per cent of people report they are flourishing in life.[5] Clearly, people everywhere are struggling, yet there are many scientifically supported things we can do to give ourselves a lift. This is what this book is about.

I am not naively suggesting that you can be a 10 out of 10 on the emotional ladder, day in, day out—no-one can. Sometimes life is tough, and we all have ups and downs. To quote the ancient wisdom of Solomon, "There is a time for everything . . . a time to weep and a time to laugh."[6] But encouragingly, research indicates that our life circumstances only contribute about 10 per cent to our level of enduring happiness.[7] This offers hope. Regardless of our life circumstances, we can discover more joy.

Studies also suggest that another 50 per cent of our enduring happiness is determined by our genetics,[8] which explains why some people are naturally cheerier than others—although

another new field of science called "epigenetics" is suggesting that our environment (nurture) may have a lot bigger part to play than genetics (nature).[9]

This leaves about 40 per cent—nearly half—of our enduring happiness that we get to choose. This book can help you choose better.

For this book to work for you, you need to go beyond merely reading—you need to apply it. At the end of each chapter, I have included ways to put the learnings into practice. I can't encourage you enough to engage with these challenges. Consider them self-experiments to test and see what works for you. As with most things in life, the more you put in, the more you will get out of it.[10]

I sincerely hope that this book helps you to live more happy.

Cheers,
Darren

1. D Morton, J Hinze, B Craig, W Herman, L Kent, P Beamish, M Renfrew and G Przybylko (In Press), "A Multimodal Lifestyle Intervention for Increasing the Mental Health and Emotional Wellbeing of College Students," *American Journal of Lifestyle Medicine*; J Hinze and D Morton (In Press), "Wellbeing Education for Educators," *TEACH Journal*.

2. J Helliwell, R Layard and J Sachs (2016), "World Happiness Report 2016," <worldhappiness.report>.

3. C G Davey and A M Chanen (2016), "The unfulfilled promise of the antidepressant medications," *Medical Journal of Australia*, 204(9), pages 248–50; C P Stephenson, E Karanges and I S McGregor (2012), "Trends in the utilisation of psychotropic medications in Australia from 2000 to 2011," *Australian and New Zealand Journal of Psychiatry*, 47(1), pages 74–87.

4. E D Kantor, C D Rehm, J S Haas, A T Chan and E L Giovannucci (2015), "Trends in Prescription Drug Use Among Adults in the United States From 1999-2012," *Journal of the American Medical Association*, 314(17), pages 1818–31.

5. B L Fredrickson and M F Losada (2005), "Positive Affect and the Complex Dynamics of Human Flourishing," *American Psychologist*, 60(7), pages 678–86.

6. See Ecclesiastes 3:1, 4.

7. J L Kurtz and S Lyubomirsky (2008), "Towards a durable happiness" in S J Lopez and J G Rettew (editors), *The Positive Psychology Perspective Series*, Vol 4, Greenwood Publishing Group, pages 21–36.

8. ibid.

9. A Menke and E B Binder (2014), "Epigenetic alterations in depression and antidepressant treatment," *Dialogues in Clinical Neuroscience*, 16(3), pages 395–404.

10. S Lyubomirsky, R Dickerhoof and J K Boehm (2011), "Becoming Happier Takes Both a Will and a Proper Way: An Experimental Longitudinal Intervention To Boost Well-Being," *Emotion*, 11(2), pages 391–402.

Chapter 1

What we need to know about our Limbo

*Men ought to know that from the brain, and from the brain
only, arise our pleasures, joy, laughter and jests.*
—Hippocrates

*I never came across any of my discoveries through the
process of rational thinking.*
—Albert Einstein

In the spirit of simplicity, let me introduce you to your
"Limbo," the nickname I have given to the part of our brain
referred to as the "Limbic system." Our Limbo contains several
structures—all with complicated names—but getting to know
it as the "Limbo" will work for our purposes. As we are about
to discover, our Limbo is an incredibly important part of us
and we want to keep it in great working order.

In case you are wondering where our Limbo lives, it is located
in the middle of our brain, just below the part that looks like a
cauliflower, which I call the "Leader."

Much has been learned about the Limbo through the work of
inquisitive brain researchers who love to push buttons and see

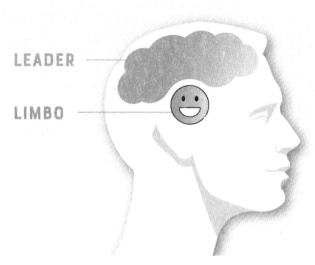

LEADER

LIMBO

what happens. They began by wiring up the Limbos of cats and rats in a way that allowed them to send a tiny electrical impulse to the area when the researchers pushed a button.

The researchers noted that if they stimulated one part of a cat's Limbo, the cat would begin to purr—and dribble, of course—become playful, and basically turn into a very happy and likeable animal.[1] Intriguingly, if they continued to stimulate this part of the cat's Limbo, it would lose all interest in food. Happy and thin—having our Limbo wired up in this way might sound appealing.

But the researchers discovered that if they moved the wires slightly and stimulated another part of the cat's Limbo, the

> **Note:** There is some debate among brain scientists regarding what structures are considered part of the Limbic system. I will assume the Limbic system includes the parahippocampal gyrus, cingulate gyrus, amygdala, hippocampus, septal nuclei, hypothalamus, olfactory system, sensory association corticies and portions of the thalamus.[2] So glad we cleared that up!

opposite reaction occurred. The cat threw a hissy fit—hackles up, claws out, even some spitting thrown in for effect. What's more, the cat would eat anything it could get its paws on. Repetitive stimulation of the cat's Limbo in this way caused them to morph into an obese, hostile fiend that was no fun to be around.

So that the rats in the laboratory didn't feel left out, the researchers also wired up their Limbos, but added another element. They gave the rats the ability to press a button so they could stimulate their own Limbo. To the amazement of the researchers, the rats repeatedly pressed the button, even in preference to eating and drinking.[3] If left unchecked, the rats would eventually die from exhaustion, their tiny paws still poised on the button attempting one more buzz.

Home of Happy—the Limbo's main role

The researchers had discovered that the Limbo is the region of the brain responsible for emotions—feeling is its core business and mood its main role. If stimulated in the right way, it made the cats and rats feel good; if stimulated in the wrong way, it made them feel bad.

Our brains are a little larger and more complex but not unlike that of rats and cats. We too have a Limbo. And like cats and rats,

Note: Over the past few decades, scientists have made incredible advances in understanding the human brain, thanks largely to sophisticated scanning technologies such as MRIs. While these studies show that the human brain is amazingly more complex than ever imagined, both in its design and connections, the Limbo is consistently implicated in mood.[4]

3

our Limbo is the part of our brain that determines how we feel—scientists even refer to it as the "emotional brain."[5] Put simply, it is our "home of happy," if we stimulate it in the right way. This is what this book is dedicated to doing—helping us discover how to stimulate our Limbo in the right way, so we can feel better and "happier" more often—more "up" and less "down"! And there are some really good reasons why we should do this.

- **Happy people have a better quality of life.**

    Think about this statement for a moment: *The quality of your emotions determines the quality of your life.*

    I am sure you will agree this is true. If you spend most of your time "up" and feeling good, life is good. If, on the other hand, you spend most of your time feeling "down" and low in mood, life is lousy.

    Note that the things in our life—relationships, circumstances, possessions and so on—are merely vehicles to emotions. If they lead to positive emotions, they contribute to our quality of life; but if they breed negative emotions, they detract from our quality of life. As much as we are able, it is good to surround ourselves with "wings" rather than "weights."

    In short, the first good reason we should endeavour to give ourselves an emotional boost is that our quality of life is better. And—as upbeat people are more fun to be around—the quality of life of those we associate with will be better as well!

- **Happy people live longer.**

    In 2001, researchers from the University of Kentucky published a fascinating study on the longevity of nuns.[6] The researchers uncovered the autobiographies of 180 nuns that had been penned when the nuns first entered the convent in the

1930s. They analysed the tone of these writings—whether they were upbeat and optimistic or forlorn and pessimistic—to see if it influenced how long they lived. It is worth noting that nuns are ideal for a study like this because their lifestyle habits are similar—similar diet and physical activity levels—and they are unlikely to do drugs or participate in other risky activities. The researchers found that fewer than one in five of the least happy nuns were still alive at the age of 93, whereas more than half of the happiest nuns were.

Similar findings have been replicated by other studies.[7] Analysing the writings of well-known deceased psychologists, researchers from the University of Kansas found that those who used more positive emotional words lived about three years longer.[8] Another study found that older individuals with a more positive outlook toward ageing lived 7.5 years longer than those who did not share the same optimistic outlook.[9]

> *Older individuals with a more positive outlook toward ageing lived 7.5 years longer than those who did not share the same optimistic outlook.*

To take it one step further, researchers from Wayne State University asked the question, "Can longevity be predicted by something as simple as how much someone smiles in a photograph?" To test it, they took 230 major league baseball cards from 1952, rated the player's "smile intensity" on the card, and mapped it against how long they lived. Remarkably, the players who pulled the cheesiest grins—described as a *Duchene* smile—lived on average seven years longer than those who didn't smile at all.[10]

A smile adding seven years of extra life is incredible, especially when we consider that eating a healthy diet, being physically active and not smoking only add about two years each to one's life expectancy.[11] Obviously, it wasn't just one smile—the smiley players in the baseball study were probably smilier most of the time. (Although, it might be worth smiling more in photos just in case.)

A little later, we will examine *why* being happy increases our life span, particularly in relation to the functioning of our immune system, but one thing is clear: Happy people tend to live longer. After reviewing many studies examining the relationship between longevity and happiness, renowned researcher Dr Ed Diener estimated that a very happy person is likely to live between four to 10 years longer than their unhappy neighbour.[12]

It seems that the ancient proverb is correct: "Being cheerful keeps you healthy; it is a slow death to be gloomy all the time."[13]

• **Happy people are more successful.**

To continue the theme of "smiling studies," one study found that the extent to which women smiled in their college yearbook photo significantly predicted their levels of wellbeing and marital satisfaction 30 years later—even after taking into consideration how physically attractive or socially desirable the women were deemed to be.[14]

The productivity benefits of happiness have been repeatedly demonstrated in the workplace.[15] Happier employees are more creative, display superior performance, are more inclined to "go the extra mile" and perform more helpful acts that translate to better customer service.[16]

Happier people also tend to be more present—in more ways

than one. First, they exhibit less absenteeism by taking fewer days off. But perhaps even more importantly, they demonstrate lower levels of "presenteeism." Do you know the feeling of "being there but not really being there"? Happy people tend to experience it less—when they are there, they are actually there! So it is hardly surprising that happy people tend to earn more—one study found as much as 30 per cent.[17] It pays to be happy!

It's obviously important to treat our Limbo well. It can affect our quality of life, our length of life and how successful we might be. But there is still more we need to know about our Limbo. While the Limbo's primary function is feeling, it also has three other important functions. As we consider them, note that these other functions are always linked to its main function, which is feeling.

> *Our Limbo can affect our quality of life, our length of life and how successful we might be.*

Memory

Do you need help with your memory at times? Do you find yourself forgetting things you should remember but remembering things you probably should forget? It is our Limbo that decides what gets filed and what gets forgotten, and it makes that decision on the basis of how it *feels*.

To illustrate, have you ever had the embarrassing experience of meeting someone for the first time only to have their name vanish from your mind moments after they have told it to you? What makes it more embarrassing is when they have clearly made a mental note of your name and insert it into every sentence at least three times: "So Darren, tell me Darren, how is your day going, Darren?"

It is awkward to ask their name again because it suggests a low care factor when we heard it the first time. In other words, if there is not strong *feeling* attached to something, we tend to forget it. This is why Dale Carnegie, author of *How to Win Friends and Influence People*, states that the sweetest sound to anyone is the sound of their own name. It communicates that we care.

On the flip side, we have no problem remembering the name of a certain someone who makes our heart flutter. I don't recall much about Grade 3—I don't remember the classroom or the teacher—but I do remember the name of the girl I had a crush on. When I got to sit next to her in story time, my heart pounded in my chest. Strong feelings promote strong memories and I remember her name to this day.

While we are on the topic of school, which teachers feature most prominently in your memory? I have two. The first had a mandatory policy to strap at least half the class each time we met, so I lived in fear of him. The second took an interest in me and nurtured me, which made me feel good about myself. I remember little of what they taught me, but I will always remember them because of the way they made me feel.

This is worth reflecting on. The thing we remember most about people is the way they make us feel. So how do we make others feel? We will be remembered—or not—for it.

The takeaway message is that our Limbo, primarily responsible for our feelings, is also in charge of our memories. If we don't feel strongly, we will likely forget; if we do feel strongly, we will likely remember. If the feelings are intense enough—such as when a terrifying event triggers a phobia—we can remember for a lifetime.

In this book, we will discover many more uncanny things about the Limbo's involvement in memory, but we are beginning to see how important this part of our brain is!

Motivation

Most of what we do, we do for a feeling, either to avoid pain or achieve pleasure. Aristotle came up with this notion thousands of years ago. The reason for this is that our Limbo—our emotional hub—is responsible for our drives. It is for this reason that feelings move us. In fact, the word "emotion" literally means "to move."

This is why fear and love—the two strongest feelings experienced by humans—are tremendous motivating forces that inspire our best efforts. Even someone who avoids exercise at all costs will find it easy to find the motivation to push themselves to levels of exhaustion they didn't know existed if they are chased by something that terrifies them! Strong feelings like love and fear can also motivate us to perform all manner of strange and sometimes embarrassing behaviours. In

> *Most of what we do, we do for a feeling, either to avoid pain or achieve pleasure.*

his book *Emotional Intelligence*, Daniel Goleman points out that smart people can do really dumb things when feelings gets involved—or, in other words, when the Limbo takes over.

For many years, I have been involved in helping people adopt healthier lifestyles and I can tell you that to achieve long-term behaviour change requires more than knowledge. The world is full of people who know what to do, but who don't do what they know. Why? Ask someone why he or she is eating a pizza the size of their head, even though they said they were going on a diet, and they will tell you, "I *feel* like it!"

Ask a couch potato why they don't get up and do something active and they will tell you, "I don't *feel* like it." They couldn't be more explicit; their Limbo isn't in the mood, so their motivation levels are low. The behaviour-change experts who wrote the book *Change Anything* advise that in order to adopt a new behaviour for good, you need to discover a way to *feel* positively about it.[18]

Clearly, mood and motivation go hand in hand, so if we are interested in discovering greater levels of motivation, we need to leverage our Limbo. As we implement the Limbo-lifting strategies in this book, don't be surprised when we discover more motivation!

Many automatic bodily processes

I know *you* are not the kind of person who exceeds the speed limit when driving a car, but we might know someone who does. Hypothetically, if *that person* were to speed down the road and then suddenly hear a siren and notice in their rearview mirror a police car with flashing lights indicating for them to pull over, they would likely experience several automatic changes within their body. Their heart would pound in their chest. Their palms would sweat. Butterflies would come alive in their stomach.

There is a strong relationship between our emotional state and many automatic bodily processes. I say "automatic bodily processes" because they occur without us having to *think* about it. In fact, *thinking* can't make our heart rate increase, palms sweat and stomach lurch, unless of course we think about something that makes us *feel*, in which case our Limbo does its work. We will learn more about this in Chapter 6.

As the Limbo has such an impact on our heart, it is not surprising that people with higher anger scores are two-and-a-half times more likely to experience a heart attack than more placid folk.[19] Similarly, the emotional stress of being exposed to heavy traffic increases the risk of a heart attack in the following hour by almost three times.[20] There are now many studies indicating that a happy Limbo helps our heart to be happy too.[21]

In case we were thinking that those butterflies in our stomach during anxious moments are harmless, think again. Researchers are discovering that there is an intimate connection between the brain and gut, as we will learn more about in Chapter 7. Scientists have discovered that approximately 70 per cent of our immune system is distributed around our gut,[22] so it is little wonder that an upset gut can influence our health in a profound way.

In a fascinating study conducted by researchers from the University of Ohio, blister wounds administered to the forearms of married couples took 30 per cent longer to heal following an animated argument with their spouse, which of course raised stress levels.[23] Similarly, wounds inflicted on the hard-palate of dental students healed 40 per cent slower in the stressful lead up to exams as compared to the low-stress summer vacation period.[24]

> *There are now many studies indicating that a happy Limbo helps our heart to be happy too.*

The takeaway message is that *how we feel affects how we heal.*

What this means is that it not only feels good to experience positive emotions, it is also *good for us*. Happiness and health go hand in hand—one promotes and complements the other—and the reason for this is the Limbo is intimately involved in both.

Hmmm, want your Limbo in a good state?

As we look over the list of the functions of the Limbo— **H**appiness, **M**emory, **M**otivation and **M**any automatic bodily

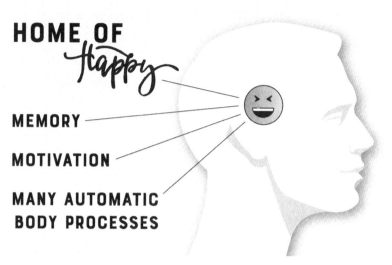

HOME OF
happy

MEMORY

MOTIVATION

MANY AUTOMATIC
BODY PROCESSES

processes—we can see that they can be represented as "Hmmm." And that is the sound I hope you are making as we consider how important it is for us to get our Limbo in the best state we can.

So how can we achieve it?

Here comes the exciting part.

Like the cats that were made friendly or ferocious simply by stimulating their Limbo in the appropriate way, we can push the buttons to stimulate our Limbo for better or worse and, in doing so, change the way we feel.

So let's learn how to stimulate our Limbo for good!

1. P MacLean and J Delgado (1953), "Electrical and chemical stimulation of the fronto-temporal portion of the limbic system in the waking animal," *Electroencephalograph Clinical Neurophysiology*, 5(1), pages 91–100.
2. D L Clark, N N Boutros and M F Mendez (2010), *The Brain and Behavior: An Introduction to Behavioral Neuroanatomy*, 3rd edition, Cambridge Press.

3. J Olds and P Milner (1954), "Positive reinforcement produced by electrical stimulation of septal area and other regions of rat brain," *Journal of Comparative and Physiological Psychology*, 47, pages 419–27.

4. W C Drevets, L Joseph, J L Price and M L Furey (2008), "Brain structural and functional abnormalities in mood disorders: Implications for neurocircuitry models of depression," *Brain Structure and Function*, 213, pages 93–118.

5. Clark, et al, op cit.

6. D D Danner, D A Snowdon and W V Friesen (2001), "Positive Emotions in Early Life and Longevity: Findings from the Nun Study," *Journal of Personality and Social Psychology*, 80(5), pages 804–13.

7. E Diener and M Y Chan (2011), "Happy People Live Longer: Subjective Well-Being Contributes to Health and Longevity," *Applied Psychology: Health and Well-being*, 3(1), pages 1–43.

8. S Pressman and D Cohen (2012), "Positive Emotion Word Use and Longevity in Famous Deceased Psychologists," *Health Psychology*, 31(3), pages 297–305.

9. B R Levy, M D Slade, S R Kunkel and S V Kasl (2002), "Longevity Increased by Positive Self-Perceptions of Aging," *Journal of Personality and Social Psychology*, 83(2), pages 261–70.

10. E Abel and M Kruger (2010), "Smile Intensity in Photographs Predicts Longevity," *Psychological Science*, 21(4), pages 542–4.

11. G Fraser and D Shavlik (2001), "Ten years of life. Is it a matter of choice?" *Archive of Internal Medicine*, 161, pages 1645–52.

12. Diener, op cit.

13. Proverbs 17:22, Good News Bible.

14. L Harker and D Keltner (2001), "Expressions of Positive Emotion in Women's College Yearbook Pictures and Their Relationship to Personality and Life Outcomes Across Adulthood," *Journal of Personality and Social Psychology*, 80(1), pages 112–24.

15. I Roberston and C Cooper (2011), *Well-being: Productivity and happiness at work*, Palgrave Macmillan.

16. J K Boehm and S Lyubomirsky (2008), "Does Happiness Promote Career Success?" *Journal of Career Assessment*, 16(1), pages 101–16; E Diener and R Biswas-Diener (2008), *Happiness: Unlocking the Mysteries of Psychological Wealth*, Blackwell Publishing.

17. Diener and Biswas-Diener, ibid.

18. K Patterson, J Grenny, D Maxfield, R McMillan and A Switzler (2011), *Change Anything: The New Science of Personal Success*, Piatkus.

19. J E Williams, C C Paton, I C Siefler, M L Eigenbrodt, F J Nieto and H A

Tyroler (2000), "Anger Proneness Predicts Coronary Heart Disease Risk: Prospective Analysis From the Atherosclerosis Risk In Communities (ARIC) Study," *Circulation*, 101, pages 2034–39.

20. A Peters, S von Klot, M Heier, I Trentinaglia, A Hörmann, H E Wichmann and H Löwel (2004), "Exposure to Traffic and the Onset of Myocardial Infarction," *New England Journal of Medicine*, 351(17), pages 1721–30.

21. J K Boehm and L D Kubzansky (2012), "The Heart's Content: The Association Between Positive Psychological Well-Being and Cardiovascular Health," *Psychological Bulletin*, 138(4), pages 655–91.

22. E Mayer (2011), "Gut feelings: the emerging biology of gut–brain communication," *Nature Reviews*, 12, pages 453–66.

23. J K Kiecolt-Glaser, T J Loving, J R Stowell, W B Malarkey, S Lemeshow, S L Dickinson and R Glaser (2005), "Hostile marital interactions, proinflammatory cytokine production, and wound healing," *Archives of General Psychiatry*, 62, pages 1377–84.

24. P T Marucha, J K Kiecolt-Glaser and M Favagehi (1998), "Mucosal wound healing is impaired by examination stress," *Psychosomatic Medicine*, 60, pages 362–5.

Introducing SMILERS—a simple acronym to help us remember the everyday things we can do to stimulate our Limbo in the best ways. Look out for this graphic at the end of each chapter as we add to it, piece by piece.

S·M·I·L·E·R·S

Chapter 2

Our Limbo is listening

—Speak positively—

*A wise, old Indian teacher instructs his grandson. "Each of us," he
says, "has two wolves within our head that fight each other. One is a
black wolf and it tells us things that bind and destroy.
The other is a white wolf that liberates and sets us free."
"Which wolf wins the fight?" asks the grandson.
The teacher replies, "The one we feed."*
—Old Cherokee Tale

*A word out of your mouth may seem of no account, but it
can accomplish nearly anything—or destroy it.*
—The Message

Let me set the scene by asking what might seem a silly
question: We have established that our Limbo is the
emotional hub of our brain—but how does it know when to
make us feel glad, bad, mad or sad?

The question is not as silly as it sounds. Our brain, including
the Limbo, has no sensation of its own—it cannot *feel* anything

15

on its own. When a surgeon operates on the brain, they have to use anaesthetic to get through the scalp and skull because skin and bones have pain receptors, but once inside and working on the brain, no anaesthetic is required. Our brain is numb! Cut it, prod it, poke it, and we won't feel a thing, which leads back to this interesting question: If our Limbo has no feelings itself, how does it know what emotion to excite and when?

The answer is that it relies on what it is told, which of course leads to the obvious question: What *tells* the Limbo how to feel?

Our Limbo is hard-wired to several other parts of our body and it receives messages from them. Follow the logic here: If we know what these sources of input to the Limbo are, we can purposefully and intentionally use them to send the messages we want our Limbo to receive and, in so doing, change our emotional state.

This is the primary focus of this book—to show where our Limbo gets its information from and how we can deliberately use these sources to send it uplifting inputs. I hope you see the potential of this to help you live more and are as excited about learning it as I am about sharing it!

So let's discover the first source of input to our Limbo.

Your language zone

Located in our higher brain, which we are referring to as the "Leader," are two areas that work together to form our speech and language. As illustrated, leading from these areas is an extensive array of nerves connecting to the Limbo.

To state it simply: Our Limbo listens to our language. Bearing this in mind, there is something else we need to know about the Limbo. Although our Limbo carries some incredible responsibilities—defining how we feel, determining

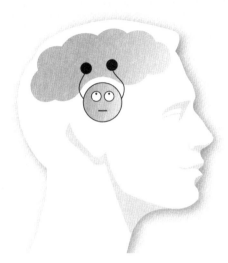

our motivation, deciphering our memory and directing many automatic bodily processes—it is highly impressionable. In fact, our Limbo can be likened to a two-year-old child in terms of its ability to think and reason. It is great at its job, but its job isn't to engage in higher-order thinking; that's the responsibility of the Leader.

Essentially, our Leader is our *thinking* brain, while our Limbo is our *feeling* brain. Like an infant relies on its guardian for leadership, our Limbo looks to the Leader for guidance.

> **Note:** Human language is an amazingly complex phenomenon. While other animals communicate with each other, we take it to an entirely new level. There are about 7000 languages spoken in the world and, on average, each day men speak around 7000 words and women about 20,000 words! Our linguistic skills are enabled by the well-developed Broca's and Wernikie's areas in our higher brain—the "Leader"—which is responsible for speech and language.

We offer this guidance every time we speak, both to ourselves and to others. So are the messages we are sending positive?

What did I say?

Most of us talk to ourselves. We just prefer not to get caught doing it. For example, I always speak to myself just before I launch off the side of a cliff in my hang-glider. Before I get in my harness, I say to myself, "OK, I have checked the glider and it all looks good. This is going to be a great flight!" Then I fasten myself in and move closer to the edge of the cliff. When the conditions feel good, I say, "Feels good." Finally, just prior to taking the first step, I say, "Clear to go!" Note that I choose my words carefully because others who hear me might think I am speaking to them, so I don't come across as crazy!

So why do I talk to myself like this? Simply because it makes me feel calmer.

I am sure you have heard this "Speak positively" message before and you might have thought it was just pop psychology. But I hope you now realise that it has merit because our brain is wired that way. Our Limbo is literally hard-wired to be influenced by language.

My hang-gliding illustration is one example of using language for good, but we often use it for bad and our emotional wellbeing suffers. If we were to constantly say things like, "Oh no, this is really, really bad!" and "I'm so useless!" around a two-year-old in our care, what emotional state would they be reduced to? They would soon become a psychological wreck. Yet many people submit their "two-year-old" Limbo to such a verbal battering on an ongoing basis. Like the old Cherokee tale at the beginning of this chapter, we feed our feelings with our words.

I see many examples of people negatively manipulating their own Limbo and reaping undesirable emotional outcomes, effectively sabotaging their own happiness. I once picked up a hitchhiker and, as he strapped himself in, I asked how he was going. Big mistake!

In a gruff tone, he replied, "Terrible! I have the worst luck. Got up this morn'n and my fridge was broken. Lost all me food and I'd just been shopp'n the day before. This stuff always happens to me! So I got in me car and it won't start. So here I am try'n to catch a ride in this scorch'n heat." He paused for a moment to take a breath, then concluded with, "And the worst thing is these things always come in threes!"

> *I see many examples of people negatively manipulating their own Limbo and reaping undesirable emotional outcomes, effectively sabotaging their own happiness.*

How do you think his Limbo was doing? As he spoke, I could imagine the "two-year-old" Limbo inside his skull saying, "We've already attracted two bad things today and another one is on its way!"

As the hitchhiker got out of my car, I said, "Good luck with that third bad thing." I was sure he would find it.

Consider another illustration. If we want to feed a fear, we simply talk it up. For example, there are few people who enjoy needles, but those who are most fearful often feed the fear through their language. They will tell you that a standard needle is "huge" or "massive." "It's as thick as my finger," they will proclaim adamantly. And it doesn't just feel like a pin prick, "It kills!" If I was a two-year-old and someone I looked up to was telling me about this horrific experience I was about to endure,

I too would be terrified. Is it any wonder their Limbo freaks out?

The point is that what we say to ourselves affects how we feel, because we are designed that way.

And it doesn't matter whether the words that ruminate in our head actually find their way to our mouth. Our Limbo still hears them because the message still gets sent from the language area of our Leader down the "wires" to our Limbo. Hence, our *internal dialogue* is also important.

It is one thing to be able to bite our tongue and even exchange pleasantries with others, but another thing entirely to take control over what is said in our internal world. Our internal dialogue can have a profound effect on how we feel.

For example, have you ever talked yourself—internally—into feeling a particular way? Perhaps you felt a little queasy in the stomach, then started to tell yourself you might be coming down with something, and ended up having to go and lie down?

There is a condition comically referred to as "medical student syndrome" in which budding doctors believe they have contracted all kinds of diseases after learning about their symptoms. They sit in class and their internal dialogue goes something like this: "I get headaches occasionally" and "Oh no, I sort of had a rash that looked a little like that." Before long, they are getting themselves checked out for all manner of ailments.

I am sure you are familiar with how easy it is to talk yourself—internally—into feeling annoyed with someone. It can start with something innocuous like them not acknowledging you when you asked them a question. The real reason they didn't respond was because they didn't hear you, but while you suspect that might have been the case, your internal dialogue gets the better of you. Words start forming in your head and your Limbo listens in attentively: "They always do that. They have absolutely no respect.

They must be annoyed with me about something and trying to make their displeasure known. Well, two can play at that game! If they want war, they picked on the wrong person!! Ahhh!!!"

It is amazing how quickly our internal dialogue can escalate. Within minutes, an unsuspecting victim can become a sworn enemy. Imagine what days and days of stewing can achieve.

Another important aspect of our internal dialogue is our explanatory style. It is human to try to make sense of life, but people differ in the way they explain life events *to themselves* and this has a big impact on both their health and happiness.[1] When optimists experience a setback, they tend to explain it to themselves as bad luck, while they attribute good outcomes to the skills and talents they possess. On the other hand, pessimists describe bad situations as their own creation and good ones as improbable fluke.

Essentially, optimists have a tendency to bombard their Limbo with uplifting words, while pessimists flood theirs with doom and gloom. Is it any wonder pessimists are characteristically portrayed as sullen and downcast, while optimists as bubbly and outgoing?

The power of words on our emotional brain is well documented. In fact, "bibliotherapy"— literally meaning "book therapy" and engaging with inspiring writings—has been shown in many studies to be highly effective for giving people an emotional lift.[2] But we don't need to read an entire book, even just a few words can affect us. Researchers from Queen's

> *Essentially, optimists have a tendency to bombard their Limbo with uplifting words, while pessimists flood theirs with doom and gloom.*

University conducted a study in which participants were asked to unscramble sentences of five words. They found that when the sentences included religious words such as "divine," they displayed more self-control—in the form of being more able to endure discomfort and delay gratification—in exercises performed shortly after.[3]

In another study, subjects were asked to unscramble seemingly random words. Some subjects were given truly random words, while another group were given words like "Florida", "Bingo" and "Gray"—words associated with the elderly. While the subjects in the study didn't make that connection, as they left the study venue, the researchers observed that they moved slower than those participants who didn't unscramble "elderly" words.[4]

These studies highlight the pervasive influence words, language and speech can have on our Limbo. The challenges at the end of this chapter will help us speak more positively, but before we get to them, it is important to know that our Limbo listens not only to what we say to ourselves, but to others as well.

Speak positively to others

I often muse over "comeback" statements. You know how it works. Someone says something degrading or demeaning to you, so you aim to level the score by firing a get-even comment back at them. We respond in this way because it feels so good, doesn't it? Or does it? Delivering a devastating comeback might be sweet in our mouth, but it often turns bitter in our belly.

Few times in my life have I been sharp enough to make a really good comeback. Usually it takes me about 24 hours to come up with something truly witty—and the moment has passed. But on the odd occasion I have pulled it off, I can't report any long-lasting emotional boost. If we are honest with ourselves, negative speech—whether directed to ourselves or to someone else—drags *us* down emotionally. It does so because our Limbo listens in on the lot.

One of the world's leading authorities on marriage is Professor John Gottman. He and his colleagues have conducted many fascinating studies and published prolifically. In one study, he could predict with nearly 90 per cent accuracy whether a newlywed couple would divorce within five years, simply by listening to how they *spoke* to and about each other in interviews.[5] His research suggested that, in order for a relationship to flourish, there needs to be at least five positive things said for every one negative.[6]

The idea of a "positivity ratio" is intriguing, and John Gottman is not the only one who has stumbled upon it. Marcial Losada studied the effectiveness of business teams and discovered that the highest-performing teams had

Speaking positively to others benefits both them and us.

the highest ratio of positive to negative interactions—the best performing teams had 5.6 positive statements for every negative one.[7] While there is some debate about the exact ratio,[8] it seems that five or more positive "speech acts" are required for every negative in order for individuals, marriages, families and even businesses to flourish. If the ratio falls below three to one, there is often impending trouble.[9]

Speaking positively to others benefits both them and us. Our Limbo gets to hear the words on the way out and their Limbo gets to hear them on the way in. So now we have learned the value of *speaking positively* and the reason why it works, it is time to experience it!

Putting it into action

Here are our two challenges, remembering that the more we put in, the more we will get out:

1. Ingrain inspiration.

We are losing a treasure from the past. We have access to information at our fingertips—we can carry around the information of hundreds of books on a device that fits into our pocket! But having something in our pocket is not the same as having it in our head. Before the advent of such technologies, people had limited access to information, so had to memorise texts and sayings. There was—and is—tremendous value to doing this.

Our first challenge is to *ingrain inspiration*—to commit to memory inspirational texts or sayings. It might be anything that is relevant to you. There are thousands of uplifting things to memorise—just search "inspirational quotes" online, if you need somewhere to begin. Write the chosen saying down on a piece of paper or type it into your phone—this is an important step toward memorising anything, especially if you are a visual learner. Practise reciting it until you know it by heart. Every time you do, your Limbo is listening.

Let it become your response to negative self-talk. When you catch yourself engaging in negative self-talk, pinch yourself and recite the inspirational text you have memorised.

I try to make a habit of memorising inspirational texts and sayings, and I have lost count of how many times I have had one pop into my head at a time I needed it. It is like we create a memory bank of wisdom for our "two-year-old" Limbo to draw from. And it does!

2. Be complimentary.

Mark Twain once wrote, "I can live for two months on a good compliment." Following that logic, he could get by on only six compliments a year. But most of us need them more frequently.

Your challenge is to be the dispenser of compliments. It is an excellent way to help you get your positivity ratio up! In one of the inspiring and quirky presentations by "Kid President" called "20 things we should say more often,"[10] he concludes with "Say something nice!" It is simple but amazingly powerful.

I often tell my children that, if you want others to like you, there is a greater and a lesser way to go about it. The lesser way is to make them feel good. The greater way is to make them feel good *about themselves*. Nothing works better at making someone feel good about themself than offering a compliment. We often think good things about others, but we say them less often. Start doing it. It doesn't need to be face-to-face if that is too scary for you. Write an email. Send a text. Test and see if it makes a difference in the way it makes *you* feel.

Recap

Like the rest of our brain, our Limbo is devoid of sensation, so it relies on incoming messages to know when to make us feel happy, sad, mad or glad. One of the sources of input to our Limbo is the language area of the Leader. Speaking positively—to both ourselves and others—can help us live more "up" and less "down"!

1. G M Buchanan and M Seligman (2013), *Explanatory Style*, Routledge Press.

2. R J Gregory, S Schwer-Canning, T W Lee and J C Wise (2004), "Cognitive Bibliotherapy for Depression: A Meta-Analysis," *Professional Psychology: Research and Practice*, 35(3), pages 275–80.

3. K Rounding, A Lee, J A Jacobson and L Ji (2012), "Religion Replenishes Self-Control," *Psychological Science*, 23, page 635.

4. J A Bargh, M Chen and L Burrows (1996), "Automaticity of Social Behavior: Direct Effects of Trait Construct and Stereotype Activation on Action," *Journal of Personality and Social Psychology*, 71(2), pages 230–44.

5. S Carrère, K T Buehlman, J M Gottman, J A Coan and L Ruckstuhl (2000), "Predicting Marital Stability and Divorce in Newlywed Couples," *Journal of Family*, 14(1), pages 42–58.

6. J M Gottman and R W Levenson (1999), "What predicts change in marital interaction over time? A study of alternative models," *Family Processes Journal*, 38(2), pages 143–58.

7. M Losada (1999), "The complex dynamics of high performance teams," *Mathematical and Computer Modelling*, 30(9–10), pages 179–92.

8. N Brown, A Sokal and H Friedman (2013), "The Complex Dynamics of Wishful Thinking: The Critical Positivity Ratio," *American Psychologist*, 68(9), pages 801–13.

9. B L Fredrickson and M F Losada (2005), "Positive affect and the complex dynamics of human flourishing," *American Psychologist*, 60(7), pages 678–86.

10. "Kid President," <www.youtube.com/watch?v=m5yCOSHeYn4>.

S·M·I·L·E·R·S

⊕ SPEAK POSITIVELY

Chapter 3

Motion creates emotion

—Move dynamically—

*Emotion is created by motion. Whatever you're feeling
right now is related to how you're using your body.*
—Anthony Robbins

Exercise is the most potent, underutilised antidepressant.
—Bill Phillips

Try this simple activity: Hold your pointer finger out in front of you as far as you can reach. With your eyes closed, guide that finger back to touch your nose. (If someone sees you doing it, just pretend you were stretching.)

So did you skillfully navigate your finger to the tip of your nose? I am assuming you did, because it actually isn't that difficult. But how is it possible given that you can't see your finger to guide it?

I once asked this question to an audience and one person said that their brain knew where their mouth was because they were constantly putting food in it, so they just aimed a little higher!

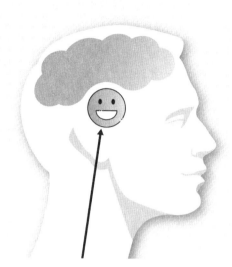

This is partly true: Our brain does know where our body parts are, even when it can't see them, because throughout our body are millions of tiny nerve endings called *proprioceptors*. Proprioceptors detect how our body is positioned and moving, then relay this information back to our brain. The sense of proprioception is so powerful: "Without it, our brains are lost."[1]

On the way to the Leader, the messages from these proprioceptors pass directly through the Limbo.[2] Like the nerves that lead from the language area of the Leader, these proprioceptors form another source of input to the Limbo. The result is that *motion creates emotion* as our proprioceptors tell our Limbo how to feel.

Act how you want to feel

Actors utilise the power of proprioception. If they have to portray an angry character, they will stomp around backstage with their fists and teeth clenched to help them get "in state." In effect, the proprioceptors send angry messages to their Limbo, so their Limbo takes the hint and gets angry. Acting how you want to feel is such a well-known tool within acting circles that "emotional states" are referred to as "actions."

Proprioceptors can be used in the same way to manage anxiety. When we are anxious, changes occur in our body, many of which—such as a racing heart and sweaty palms—we have no control over. However, we can modify symptoms of anxiety and we can use these to calm our Limbo by sending it soothing messages via our proprioceptors. These anxiety-reducing quick fixes can be summarised as the 3-S approach:

Slow refers to breathing. Anxiety is associated with shallow and rapid breathing. In fact, breathing like this can bring on an anxiety attack! Conversely, when we are calm, our breathing is slow and deep. Step one in creating a state of calmness is to consciously take slow and full breaths. This sends calming messages to the Limbo from the proprioceptors in our body. This is why breathing exercises are integral to many relaxation strategies.

> **Note:** The benefits of deep breathing were recognised and promoted more than a century ago by Ellen White, a prominent 19th-century health reformer and educator. She recommended that breathing exercises be taught even to children because such exercises are effective for "not only refreshing the body, but soothing and tranquilising the mind."[3]

Sip refers to wetting our mouth with water. Have you ever noticed how dry your mouth gets when you are anxious? You couldn't spit if your life depended on it! When I go hang-gliding,

I always have a water bottle handy and whenever I feel nervous, I take a sip. Simply wetting my mouth calms me through my proprioceptors' influence on the Limbo. If you have a fear of public speaking, take small sips of water before you get up to speak.

Sink relates to what we do with our muscles. When gripped by fear or anxiety, our muscles tighten, ready for action. This "over-excitation" is what can create the shakes when we are frightened. By making a conscious effort to relax our muscles, lowering our shoulders, wiggling our fingers and allowing our body to *sink*, we send calming messages to our Limbo via our proprioceptors.

> **Test for yourself** and see if the 3-S approach helps you feel more calm and relaxed: Take a couple of deep slow breaths, wet your mouth (if you have water nearby), and consciously relax your muscles as you sink into your seat. It really works!

Proprioceptors are known to be so powerful that even just the proprioceptors in our face can influence how we feel. In the 1970s, a researcher from Clark University explored a phenomenon referred to as "facial feedback" by placing electrodes on people's faces and stimulating their facial muscles to pull smiles or frowns.[4] Even though they didn't know what their faces were doing, participants reported "feeling more angry when frowning and more happy when smiling."

Other researchers have found that when people were forced to smile by holding a pencil in their mouth—try it!—they found watching a video clip or cartoon funnier, which made them laugh more and feel happier.[5] As Vietnamese peace activist Thich Nhat

Hanh said, "Sometimes your joy is the source of your smile, but sometimes your smile can be the source of your joy."

The takeaway message is that what we do with our body can have a profound effect on our Limbo. Former president of the American Psychological Association, Dr Martin Seligman has urged that "at least half of positive psychology occurs below the neck."[6]

Knowing that *motion creates emotion* provides an excellent opportunity for us to change our emotional state. Unfortunately, many of us are not acting in our own best interest. But we can purposefully use the proprioceptors distributed throughout our body to trick our two-year-old-like Limbo into creating the emotions we want. It's a simple principle: *Act how you want to feel.*

Don't just sit there!

Researchers from the University of Auckland in New Zealand conducted an intriguing study in which they strapped participants with tape so that they were forced into either a slumped or upright seated posture to see how it affected their mood and stress levels.[7] The participants remained in this posture for about half an hour while the researchers conducted a series of tests. Compared to those with the slumped posture, the "upright" participants reported a significant mood lift, as well as feeling more motivated, less fearful and more confident. During the experiment, the participants were asked to write a speech, and the "slumped" participants used more negative and sad words.

If you want to feel depressed, act like it in the way you position your body and the feeling will grow on you. It is my belief that part of the reason we have an epidemic of depression today is because many people are acting like they are depressed for hours and hours every day. An increasing number of people spend much of their day hunched over a computer, shoulders slumped forward and head downcast. A posture like that causes our millions of proprioceptors to send depressive signals to our Limbo. Is it any wonder that our Limbo makes us feel lousy if that is how we have spent the day?

There is nothing wrong with lazing about from time to time, but the problem is that we tend to do so much sitting nowadays, which leads to slumping. It is not uncommon for people to be "bottom-dwelling" for 15 or more hours every day,[8] which is truly remarkable given that most people are only awake for 16 to 18 hours. We sit to eat breakfast, we sit to commute to work, we sit hunched-over in front of a computer at work, we sit to commute home, we sit for dinner and then, because we are so exhausted, we sit in front of a screen until bed time, so we can do it all again the next day.

There are two things that we can do to help prevent our Limbo getting the message that we are "down" so that it doesn't make us feel more that way.

First, when seated, sit up straight with good posture. I once attended a media training course and one of the first things they taught was that when being interviewed—even if on radio, where the listeners cannot see you—sit up straight and lean forward slightly. Why? Because this posture makes us come across more energetic and animated. In effect, our proprioceptors bombard our Limbo with the message that we are alive and well, so we feel that way and come across that way to others.

Second, stand up! Historically, National Physical Activity guidelines only provided guidance as to how long and how hard we should exercise for good health. Now they also warn against "sedentary behaviours" like too much sitting. It is recommended that people should get on their feet for a few minutes every hour or so, to break up prolonged periods of sitting.[9]

The takeaway lesson is to pay careful attention to our posture.

To give our Limbo a lift, sit up and stand up! Not only will we feel better, we might discover other benefits too. A study conducted at Harvard Business School found that adopting an open, expansive posture for just two minutes before giving a speech as part of a job interview resulted in the interviewers rating the interviewee as more confident and employable.[10]

But there is an even better way to activate our proprioceptors for good effect.

Move more

Walking in my local shopping mall a while ago, I was confronted with a sign advertising "Happiness, Only $99." Thinking it was a good deal, I approached the shop assistant to inquire. He explained that the $99 was the first of 10 payments that purchased the treadmill the sign was attached to. So was it false advertising? Can exercise make us happy?

I can honestly say that exercise does make me happy and more emotionally upbeat. And the science agrees with me!

I know others who do not share my perspective but I can honestly say that exercise does make me happy and more emotionally upbeat. And the science agrees with me![11]

When we *move dynamically*, millions of proprioceptors throughout our body scream out to our Limbo, telling it that we are all-systems-go! Little wonder that being physically active can improve our mood. Just in case you remain unconvinced, here is the evidence.

We have known for decades that a single bout of exercise can lift the blues and improve mood.[12] It can take as little as 10 minutes[13] and even works for people who are suffering with major depression.[14] To date, more than 25 rigorous studies have concluded that regular physical activity is associated with better mood and the prevention of depression[15]—in other words, it can make you happier and more emotionally resilient! Studies have even shown that exercise is comparable to antidepressant medication for relieving depression[16]—and the only side-effects of exercise are good ones.

A recent study in 15 European countries found a positive association between the amount of physical activity people performed and how happy they were.[17] In other words, when it comes to physical activity, the more the merrier! Another recent study of more than 10,000 individuals revealed that not only are people who are more physically active happier, individuals are happier in the moments when they are more physically active.[18]

I hope you are now convinced and impressed by the power of "moving" to help us be up more and down less. But notice the strategy for giving our Limbo a lift introduced in this chapter is "move *dynamically.*" Studies indicate that more intense exercise is especially effective for achieving a mood lift.[19]

The reason for this is apparent: More intense exercise results in our proprioceptors cheering with a louder voice and our Limbo listens! A great way to stimulate our proprioceptors in a dynamic way is to perform resistance exercises, which are known to be very effective for making people feel good.[20] However, it is important to note that, while more intense exercise confers extra benefits, even lower-intensity physical activity works wonders.

It has been hypothesised that physical activity has depression-relieving effects partly because it promotes the development of new brain cells in our Limbo.[21] What we definitely know is that physical activity causes the Limbo to release chemicals called beta-endorphins into the rest of our brain. Beta-endorphins make us feel good—even euphoric—and can blunt pain.[22]

Ever heard of the "runner's high"? That's endorphins.[23] Interestingly, endorphins are even addictive, which is why regular exercisers get cranky if they can't get out for a few days—they are experiencing "withdrawal symptoms." My wife has kindly said to me more than once, "Darren, I think you need to go for a run!"

Recognising this, it is alarming that, over the past century, we have been witnessing an accelerating decline in our physical activity levels. Today, we are probably more inactive than humans have ever been throughout history. As you can see in the figure below, it is estimated that we are 60–70 per cent less active than those living just a few generations ago,[24] which equates to walking about 16 kilometres (10 miles) less every day. Of course, this is contributing to the current

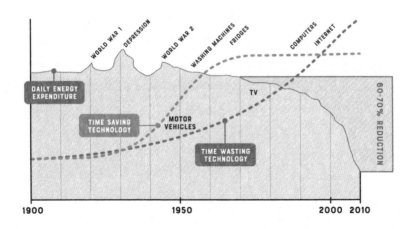

obesity epidemic and the rise in chronic diseases that we are observing, but imagine what it is doing to our Limbo. It is hardly surprising that so many people are feeling down.

> **To summarise:** Physical activity is one of the most evidence-based and effective methods available for promoting and enhancing emotional wellbeing.

Mustering motivation

But even when we know that physical activity lifts our Limbo, we can still struggle to find the motivation to do anything about it. The problem with having to move is that we have to move to do it!

Most people already know that physical activity is good for them, yet they find it difficult to follow through and do it. As the saying goes, the world is full of people who know what to do but who don't do what they know. For this reason, in my book *Live More Active*—a book dedicated to helping people activate their life for good—half the chapters are about discovering motivation.

People often say they are too exhausted to do any physical activity. They get home at the end of the day and just want to collapse in a heap on the sofa. *Running* a bath is the only exercise they feel they have the energy for. If you work as a manual labourer, you are probably forgiven for feeling that way because you might have expended a lot of energy throughout the day. But it is my observation that manual labourers are often not the ones lazing about after work; it's more likely those who have sedentary occupations.

So how do we muster the motivation to get mobile? As we now know from Chapter 1, the secret to becoming more motivated lies in switching on our Limbo, as it is also our motivation centre.

Current physical activity guidelines recommend that adults, both young and old, should be physically active for at least 30 minutes most days.[25] This doesn't mean 30 minutes of exhausting and sweaty exercise, running down the street like you just stole something. The guidelines refer to 30 minutes of *moderate-intensity* physical activity, which is what you would rate as a 3 to 4 out of 10 in effort.[26] This is not so hard! When performing moderate-intensity physical activity, we notice we are breathing a little more than normal but we can still hold a conversation.

Often when I give presentations on becoming more physically active and I share with the audience that they should aim for 30 minutes every day, I see some people adopt a facial expression that screams, "Are you kidding? Thirty minutes!" When I observe this, I change tack and

> *Once we have started to move dynamically, the messages sent by our proprioceptors cause our Limbo to get in the mood and make us feel more motivated.*

instead say that they only need to go for five minutes. When I see the relief on their faces, I conclude with, "And if after the five minutes of being active, you feel like it, go for another 25 minutes."

You have probably experienced it yourself: The hard part is getting started. Once we have started to *move dynamically*, the messages sent by our proprioceptors cause our Limbo to get in the mood and make us feel more motivated.

So if we find ourselves exhausted at the end of the day but we haven't been expending much physical energy throughout it, there is a good chance that our Limbo just needs a kick-start and we can supply it by taking the first step. To borrow the famous slogan, "Just do it!" Simply put on your walking shoes and walk to the end of your street. You have my permission to reassess whether you want to continue from there, but I will almost guarantee that your Limbo will have woken up by then. To get on a roll, we simply need to start rolling!

Putting it into action

1. Sit up and stand up.

Take note of your posture throughout the day. If you spend a lot of time sitting in front of a computer screen, are you sitting upright or slumped over? Simply adjusting the height of your screen can help achieve a better posture.

And don't sit there too long! If you are required to sit, endeavour to get up and move about for a few minutes every hour—go and get a drink of water or find any excuse to get on your feet. Standing desks, which allow you work while standing up, are a great way to decrease your sit time.

2. Step up!

Prioritise 30 minutes—or more—a day to perform moderate-intensity physical activity. Remember, it doesn't need to be hard, just a 3 to 4 out of 10 in effort. Or you can break it up into three chunks of 10 minutes as that is all it takes to give your Limbo a lift. In fact, I would encourage you to do this as you can then experience several Limbo lifts throughout the day!

If you have a step-counter such as a pedometer or electronic activity bracelet, another way to help you move more is to monitor your steps. Studies show that when people wear a pedometer, they will usually take an extra 2000 or so steps each day because there is something rewarding about watching the count go up![27] The goal is to achieve 10,000 steps each day—if you do, you are considered to be in the "active" range.[28]

3. Lift it!

Try a resistance exercise routine. For some handy tips for easy workouts at home, visit <https://vimeo.com/52790210>.

> ## Recap
> By *moving dynamically*, we can send uplifting messages to our Limbo via the millions of nerves—called proprioceptors—distributed throughout our body. So sit up, stand up and move more to live more!

1. A Abbott (2006), "In search of the sixth sense," *Nature*, 44, pages 125–7.
2. J LeDoux (1998), *The Emotional Brain*, Phoenix.
3. E White (1903), *Education*, Review and Herald.
4. J Laird (1974), "Self-attribution of emotion: the effects of expressive behavior on the quality of emotional experience," *Journal of Personality and Social Psychology*, 29(4), pages 475–86.
5. R Soussignan (2002), "Duchenne smile, emotional experience, and autonomic reactivity: A test of the facial feedback hypothesis," *Emotion*, 2(1), pages 52–74; F Strack, S Stepper and L Martin (1988), "Inhibiting and Facilitating Conditions of the Human Smile: A Nonobtrusive Test of the Facial Feedback Hypothesis," *Journal of Personality and Social Psychology*, 54(5), pages 768–77.

6. M Seligman (2011), *Flourish: A visionary new understanding of happiness and wellbeing*, Simon & Schuster, page 69.

7. S Nair, M Sagar, J Sollers, N Consedine and E Broadbent (2015), "Do slumped and upright postures affect stress responses? A randomised trial," *Health Psychology*, 34(6), pages 632–41.

8. National Heart Foundation of Australia (2016), "Sitting less for adults," <https://heartfoundation.org.au/images/uploads/publications/PA-Sitting-Less-Adults.pdf>.

9. Department of Health (2016), <www.healthyactive.gov.au>; <www.health.gov.au/internet/main/publishing.nsf/content/health-pubhlth-strateg-phys-act-guidelines>.

10. A J Cuddy, C A Wilmuth and D R Carney (2012), "The benefit of power posing before a high-stakes social evaluation," *Harvard Business School Working Paper*, No 13–027, <http://nrs.harvard.edu/urn-3:HUL.InstRepos:9547823>.

11. T Josefsson, M Lindwall and T Archer (2014), "Physical exercise intervention in depressive disorders: Meta-analysis and systematic review," *Scandinavian Journal of Medicine & Science in Sports*, 24, pages 259–72.

12. R Yeung (1996), "The acute benefits of exercise on mood state," *Journal of Psychosomatic Research*, 40(2), pages 123–41.

13. C J Hansen, L C Stevens and J R Coast (2001), "Exercise duration and mood state: How much is enough to feel better?" *Health Psychology*, 20(4), pages 267–75.

14. J B Bartholomew, D Morrison and J T Ciccolo (2005), "Effects of Acute Exercise on Mood and Well-Being in Patients with Major Depressive Disorder," *Medicine & Science in Sports & Exercise*, 37(12), pages 2032–7.

15. G Mammen and G Faulkner (2013), "Physical Activity and the Prevention of Depression. A Systematic Review of Prospective Studies," *American Journal of Preventive Medicine*, 45(5), pages 649–57.

16. J A Blumenthal, M A Babyak, K A Moore, W E Craighead, S Herman, P Khatri, R Waugh, M A Napolitano, L M Forman, M Appelbaum, P M Doraiswamy and K R Krishnan (1999), "Effects of exercise training on older patients with major depression," *Archive of Internal Medicine*, 159, pages 2349–56; G Stathopoulou, M B Powers, A C Berry, J A Smits and M W Otto (2006), "Exercise Interventions for Mental Health: A Quantitative and Qualitative Review," *Clinical Psychology: Science and Practice*, 13, pages 179–93; J A Blumenthal, M A Babyak, P M Doraiswamy, L Watkins, B M Hoffman, K A Barbour, S Herman, E Craighead, A L Brosse, R Waugh, A Hinderliter and A Sherwood (2007), "Exercise and Pharmacotherapy in the Treatment of Major Depressive Disorder," *Psychosomatic Medicine*, 69(7), pages 587–96.

17. J Richards, X Jiang, P Kelly, J Chau, A Bauman and D Ding (2015), "Don't worry, be happy: Cross-sectional associations between physical activity and happiness in 15 European countries," *BMC Public Health*, 15, page 53.

18. N Lathia, G M Sandstrom, C Mascolo and P J Rentfrow (2017), "Happier People Live More Active Lives: Using Smartphones to Link Happiness and Physical Activity," *PLoS ONE*, 12(1), e0160589.

19. N A Singh, T M Stavrinos, Y Scarbek, G Galambos, C Liber and M A Fiatarone Singh (2005), "A Randomized Controlled Trial of High Versus Low Intensity Weight Training Versus General Practitioner Care for Clinical Depression in Older Adults," *Journal of Gerontology*, 60(6), pages 768–76; R Stanton, P Reaburn and B Happell (2013), "Is Cardiovascular or Resistance Exercise Better to Treat Patients With Depression? A Narrative Review," *Issues in Mental Health Nursing*, 34, pages 531–38.

20. ibid.

21. C Ernst, A K Olson, J P Pinel, R W Lam and B R Christie (2006), "Antidepressant effects of exercise: Evidence for an adult-neurogenesis hypothesis?" *Journal of Psychiatry & Neuroscience*, 31(2), pages 84–92.

22. H Boecker (2008), "The Runner's high: opiodergic mechanisms in the human brain," *Cerebral Cortex*, 18(11), pages 1–9; A S Sprouse-Blum, G Smith, D Sugai and F D Parsa (2010), "Understanding Endorphins and Their Importance in Pain Management," *Hawaii Medical Journal*, 69, pages 70–1.

23. Boecker, op cit.

24. N Vogels, G Egger, G Plasqui and K R Westerterp (2004), "Estimating Changes in Daily Physical Activity Levels over Time: Implication for Health Interventions from a Novel Approach," *International Journal of Sports Medicine*, 25, pages 607–10.

25. Department of Health, ibid.

26. K Norton, L Norton and D Sadgrove (2010), "Position statement on physical activity and exercise intensity terminology," *Journal of Science and Medicine in Sport*, 13, pages 496–502.

27. D M Bravata, C Smith-Spangler, V Sundaram, A L Gienger, N Lin, R Lewis, C D Stave, I Olkin and J R Sirard (2007), "Using Pedometers to Increase Physical Activity and Improve Health: A Systematic Review," *Journal of the American Medical Association*, 298(19), pages 2296–304.

28. C Tudor-Locke, Y Hatano, R P Pangrazi and M Kang (2008), "Revisiting 'How many steps are enough?'" *Medicine & Science in Sports & Exercise*, 40(7), pages S537–43.

S·M·I·L·E·R·S

 MOVE DYNAMICALLY

Chapter 4

Blue and green should often be seen

—Immerse in an uplifting *physical* environment—

The further you get from nature, the less happy you are.
—George Adams

The best remedy for those who are afraid, lonely or unhappy is to go outside, somewhere where they can be quiet, alone with the heavens, nature and God.—Anne Frank

Christmas Day, 1977—when I was a tender seven years old—was memorable for me. Not in a good way.

It started well. I woke up to find a bright-green bike under the Christmas tree with my name on it! Of course, I could hardly contain my excitement and desperately wanted to take the new machine for a ride, but it was raining heavily outside. I waited and waited. But, by midday, it was clear that the rain had set in.

So, encouraged by my mum, I decided the maiden voyage would have to be a lap of the hallway in our house.

Before proceeding with the story, I need to set the scene by adding that I was wearing (only) the new Superman underwear that I had also received as a gift that unforgettable Christmas. Trust me, it's an important detail of the story.

As I was poised with my bare foot on the pedal, about to push off, something completely unexpected and alarming happened. From the ceiling above me fell the biggest and hairiest spider I have ever seen. While huntsman spiders are purportedly harmless, I still maintain that their name implies otherwise.

The hairy monstrosity landed directly on my naked knee and prepared itself for the crazy ride that was about to ensue. The moment I caught sight of it on my bare skin, I freaked out—that I was wearing Superman underwear did nothing for my courage! I leapt from the bike, completely unconcerned about damaging it, and began to convulse like a crazy person. Eventually the spider was launched from my knee through the air, but the moment it landed, it made a mad sprint for my bare foot. The craziness commenced again as I thrashed my leg about until I was freed at last.

The reason I remember that experience so well is because it was so emotionally charged and, as we learned in Chapter 1, that is how our Limbo is wired to work—strong feelings equal strong memories. But the point of the story is that sights can have instant emotional responses and they have this effect because of the way they affect the Limbo.

Even though the Limbo sits in a comfortable cranium away from the world "outside," it still knows what is happening "out there" because it receives messages from the surrounding environment. Our Limbo is constantly tuning in to and picking up cues—sights, sounds and smells—from the environment around us. Accordingly, the physical environment we are immersed in can have a profound affect on our Limbo and hence our emotional state, even without us recognising and being consciously aware of it. In this chapter, we explore how our Limbo is wired to our senses and how we can deliberately send uplifting messages to our Limbo so we can feel more upbeat.

Sight

The eye is a marvellous creation and, for most people, sight is their dominant sense. But when our optic nerves send messages from our retinas to our brain so we can "see," the messages first go to the Limbo, then to the Leader. Hence, our emotional reaction to a sight or image precedes our thinking response.

For example, if a *so-called* friend places a plastic spider on our shoulder, notice the order of our reaction. First comes an emotional "Ahhhh!" as our Limbo "sees" it, followed a moment later by "Ohhhh" as our Leader—our thinking brain—receives the signal and realises it is a fake. Indeed, our Limbo is highly influenced by sights and, because of the way it is wired, its reaction to sights can be almost instant.

Research shows that our Limbo really likes the sight of natural environments. Studies involving functional magnetic resonance imaging (fMRI) have shown that scenes of natural landscapes light up parts of the Limbo associated with positivity,[1] even when the scenes are flashed up in front of someone for only 1/100th of a second.[2] This is so fast we probably wouldn't consciously notice it! This goes to show how profoundly perceptive our Limbo is of the world around us. In contrast, city scenes increase activity in the part of the Limbo associated with

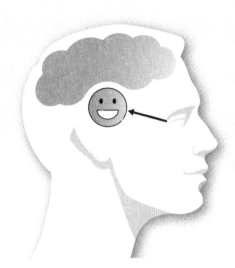

threat and stress.[3] As our Limbo is also our motivation centre, it is not unexpected that views of natural environments are linked to better performance in the workplace[4] and enhanced academic performance in schools.[5]

One critical aspect of the images that enter our eyes that influences how they affect our Limbo is their colour. Sometimes when I run or ride around the bush trails near my home, I will see a red-bellied black snake. The snakes are black on top but, when they get agitated, they rear up to show their red underbelly. When I see that red, I know it is a good time to clear out and my Limbo moves me to do just that!

The colour red is associated with danger, so our emotional response is fear and anger—essentially it commands a fight-or-flight response.[6] It is not surprising that we associate anger with "seeing red" and studies have shown that red tends to make people more vigilant, less likely to take risks and more motivated to avoid things.[7] Other colours can produce different emotional responses. For example, blue tends to make people more open, peaceful and creative.[8] Indeed, colours can affect our mood and behaviours in ways that we are often consciously unaware of.[9]

What do you think is the most cheerful, mood-lifting colour? To test this, researchers invited individuals to paint a wall in a white bedroom a colour that would make them feel more positive.[10] Overwhelmingly, the participants in the study opted for bright hues of yellow and orange. You are probably not surprised by this; yellow is commonly associated with being happy. But the reason why this is the case goes deeper than you might realise.

Essentially, your Limbo loves bright light.

In countries of high latitude, where there are extended periods of low lighting during the winter months, it is more common for people to become depressed and suicidal[11]—a condition referred to as Seasonal Affective Disorder, or "SAD" for short. On the flip side, exposing our eyes to bright light is used as a treatment for depression.[12] In fact, a recent study found that "light therapy" was more effective for relieving depression than antidepressant medications.[13]

Importantly, light therapy doesn't involve burning out our retinas by staring into the sun. So don't do that! All that is needed is for our eyes to spend time in a well-lit area.

However, the sun does seem to be the best source to light up our Limbo. Indoor light, such as that in an office environment, is typically less that 500 LUX—LUX is simply a measurement of the intensity of light. Comparably, natural sunlight can beam up to 100,000 LUX. Even on an *overcast* day, the light outside is a minimum of 1000 LUX—at least twice as bright as most indoor spaces. In the shade on a bright sunny day, we can be immersed in up to 25,000 LUX—about 50 times brighter than most indoor spaces. We might not notice, but our Limbo notices!

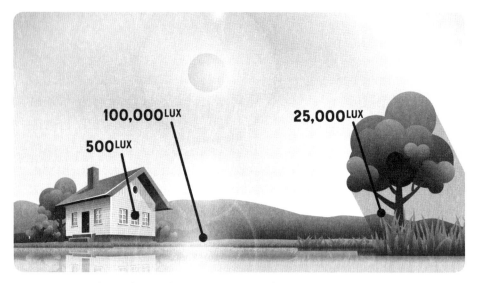

Researchers from the University of Colorado monitored how much light individuals were exposed to on a typical day in their electrically lit environment and compared it to when they went camping for a week *in winter*. They discovered that, during waking hours, the participants were, on average, exposed to light levels 13 times higher when camping as compared to when back home in the artificially lit environment—more than 10,000 versus 750 LUX.[14]

So why all this talk about LUX? The consensus is that we need about 10,000 LUX for 30 minutes each day[15]—or longer periods of exposure if the light intensity is lower—to give our Limbo a lift and feel emotionally upbeat. Researchers have also discovered that morning light seems to be especially good[16] as it has a blue tinge, because its wavelength is shorter.[17] Again, we don't notice it at a conscious level but our Limbo notices. It equates blue-tinged light with morning time, so kicks us in to "rise and shine" mode and we feel more awake and alert.

The takeaway message is that the sights we are exposed to— the images, colours and especially the brightness—can have a pronounced effect on our Limbo and then how we feel, even without us being aware of it.

> **Note:** You can buy light boxes that are used as a therapy for depression.[18] But if you have access to the sun, why not make use of it?

Sound

Our Limbo is wired for sound. Like our optic nerve, our auditory nerve sends messages directly to the Limbo. Hence, sounds can evoke all kinds of emotions[19]—hearing a scream evokes fear, listening to running water can make us feel relaxed, and the sound of a dripping tap can drive us mad!

We can all attest to the ability of music—sounds strung together—to move us emotionally. This has been recognised since biblical times when it was recorded that David would play music for King Saul to help him "feel better." Certainly, rousing music can make us feel more emotionally upbeat. One study found that the composition titled "Rodeo" by Copland is especially good for this.[20] If you don't use music to help give you a lift or relax when needed, give it a try.

Music has such an impact on our Limbo that not only are our emotions affected, all its other functions are enhanced as well. Recall from Chapter 1 that the Limbo has three functions in addition to being our emotional hub—it also plays a key role in memory, motivation and many automatic bodily process.

Consider the ability of music to enhance our memory. How many songs can you sing along to as they are randomly played on the radio? Hundreds? Possibly thousands? That is a lot of

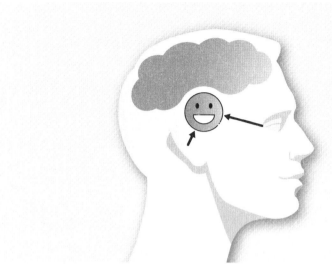

lyrics to remember. So how and why do we do it? We forget things like our wedding anniversary or phone number, but we can fluently recite the *Sesame Street* song! The reason this happens is that when our Limbo comes across a tune it likes, all its functions—including memory—are heightened. So it is not surprising that music can be used to enhance learning.[21]

Music also has the ability to make us feel more motivated, if the beat is right. This is why gyms always have upbeat music playing, to help people get in the mood. Athletes often listen to upbeat music to help them get "psyched" for an event. On the other hand, certain music can make us feel calm and relaxed, again if it is of the right kind. One study showed that listening to relaxing music before surgery reduced patients' anxiety levels better than medications.[22]

Finally, music has also been shown to alter automatic bodily processes. It is perhaps not surprising that the right kind of music can lower our heart rate and blood pressure,[23] but music composed by Mozart has even been shown to boost the immune system and reduce allergic reactions.[24] This has been referred to as the "Mozart effect" because the same immune boost doesn't seem to occur when listening to other composers—not even Beethoven! Given its influence on our automatic bodily processes, it is understandable that music has been used as medicine for thousands of years.[25]

All this evidence reinforces the fact that our Limbo responds to and is highly influenced by sounds. But there is still another sense that can have a surprisingly potent effect on our Limbo.

Smell (and taste)

While the emotional responses to sight and sound are obvious, our sense of smell is often underplayed. Smell can profoundly stimulate our Limbo because our olfactory nerve, responsible for this sense, leads from the back of our nose *directly* to our Limbo.[26] There was a time when the Limbo was referred to as the "rhinencephalon," which literally means "smell brain,"[27] because the olfactory nerve is such a massive input to the Limbo.

This explains several interesting phenomena. For example, have you ever noticed that the slightest whiff of a particular scent can instantly bring memories flooding back and transport you back in time? Our Limbo is so strongly tuned in to our sense of smell that it picks up on the scent and thinks, *I know that smell*, and proceeds to replay its associated memories. More so, it can make us *feel* like we did back then, dredging up the associated emotions. We might even experience the same automatic bodily responses we had at the time the memory was made.

For me, the smell of coconut oil reminds me of the beach in summer when I was a teenager. That was the scent of the most popular sunscreen lotion at the time, so whenever I encounter

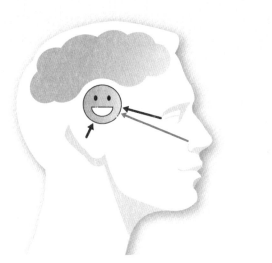

this smell, a flood of memories return and I feel carefree. I can even feel the warmth of the sun on my skin. This is a great example of the Limbo being stimulated and linking its various functions: memory, emotion and automatic bodily processes. Similarly, I have a friend who says that every time he smells burnt toast it reminds him strongly of sitting at his Grandma's kitchen table when he was a kid. Obviously Grandma wasn't such a great cook!

Smell has a sister sense: taste. You might have noticed that when your nose is blocked and you can't smell, you can't taste anything either. This explains why our emotional state can have such a strong impact on our eating habits. When our Limbo latches on to a smell or taste that it finds appealing, it keeps us coming back for more—in other words, we are highly *motivated*.

Have you ever been to an "all-you-can-eat" restaurant and proceeded to really get full value? As we sit at the table, full to the point of pain, we make a commitment that we will never again indulge like this. But a moment later we are reaching for

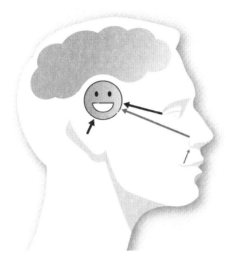

another spoonful of dessert! Why would we do such a thing to ourselves? The answer is our Limbo likes the hit it gets from our olfactory nerve and it drives us back for more. The "two-year-old" Limbo often gets its way, regardless of what the Leader might say!

Or do you notice that when we are feeling down we tend to repetitively open the refrigerator door or the cookie jar and devour what lies inside? It is called *comfort eating* and it is a result of our Limbo seeking a pleasurable lift in the most powerful and instantaneous way it knows—from the olfactory nerve. Boredom, which is a lack of emotional stimulation, can have a similar effect. When our "two-year-old" Limbo starts screaming, "I'm bored, I'm bored," it drives us to eat some pleasant-tasting food for stimulation. We might find ourselves absent-mindedly standing in front of the open pantry, asking ourselves, "What was I doing again?" Indeed, any change to our emotional state—including depression, stress or boredom—can affect our eating behaviours because of the way our Limbo is linked to our sense of smell and taste.

Through their effect on our Limbo, sights, sounds and smells (and tastes) can affect our mood in profound ways. Now that we are armed with these insights, let's piece it all together to explore how we can use this understanding to be more emotionally up!

The Great Outdoors are Great!

I love to hang glide. My personal height record is about 4000 metres (about 13,000 feet). To get that high, you first launch off the side of a cliff, then go hunting for an invisible pocket of rising hot air called a "thermal." Thermals are released from the ground when it gets hot in much the same way that a bubble is released from the bottom of a pot of boiling water. When you fly into a thermal, you certainly know about it because its turbulence can toss you around like a leaf in the wind. Once you have located the thermal, you then need to pluck up the courage to start turning circles inside it and hang on tight as you climb toward the heavens. The day I attained my personal height record, I watched the ground fall away as I circled up at more than 300 metres (more than 1000 feet) per minute.

When the thermal gets high enough and cold enough, it begins to condense and this gives birth to a cumulous cloud. On the day I achieved my personal height record, the air around me began to grow misty as I approached 4000 metres and I was immersed in a new creation as the sky welcomed another fluffy decoration. For several minutes, I flew around the edge of the forming cloud, just soaking it all in. The view was absolutely breathtaking, whichever way I looked. I was surrounded by bright blue and below me was a mat of green that extended to the horizon. All my senses were alert, captivated, attuned to everything around me. And it wasn't only the sights. There was a loud silence. And the moist cool air had the smell and texture

of new rain. I felt truly alive and energised—full of awe, wonder and joy—and I felt that way for days after. The experience will always stay with me.

Natural environments can lift us emotionally in rich and profound ways.[28] Surely you have already experienced it for yourself. The view from a mountain peak. Gazing out over the vast ocean as the sun sets. The sound of running water from a mountain stream. The crisp smell of an Alpine forest in the early morning or a field laden with wildflowers in spring.

Our Limbo comes alive in these natural places because of the way it is wired to our senses of sight, sound and smell. Thousand of years ago, Aristotle proposed the idea that we are designed to inhabit such places and that doing so is good for our happiness—it provides us with a "love of life" more recently referred to as *biophilia*.[29] More than 30 studies have examined the influence of exposure to natural environments on how people feel, and the consensus is that they do indeed make people feel more positive and less negative.[30]

Alarmingly, many people today live in artificial environments such as the concrete jungles of the city—"grey spaces"—and are starved of the natural world—"blue and green spaces"—that makes our Limbo come alive. A new term has even been coined: Nature Deficit Disorder. Children suffering Nature Deficit Disorder, who don't get to regularly surround themselves in the great outdoors, are more prone to anxiety, depression and attention deficit disorder.[31]

But we don't have to live in a city to be separated from nature. Many people living in rural environments are missing the benefits of the natural landscapes that exist in their own backyard because we are increasingly living our lives indoors.

One hundred years ago, Sir John Thompson warned that increasing modernisation would disconnect us from natural environments and that we would suffer for it.[32] He couldn't have been more correct. As our work, socialisation and recreation has become increasingly screen-based, we have become more disconnected from nature. Not surprisingly, a large study conducted in the United States found a significant relationship between depression and media use.[33]

It is time to reverse this trend and go *au naturel*—by which I mean return to natural environments, clothed of course. Dr Stephen Kaplan from the University of Michigan explains that modern living makes high demands of our information-processing skills—we have computers, traffic, smart phones, so many things bombarding our brains, which lead to unnatural mental strain.[34] On the other hand, natural stimuli, such as landscapes and animals, effortlessly engage our attention, so lead to less mental fatigue.[35]

Indeed, the great outdoors can do us good emotionally and there is strong evidence for this. Hospital patients who merely have a view of a natural landscape tend to consume less painkilling medication and have shorter hospital stays.[36] Exposure to "green" areas has been associated with less aggression and even just a window view of nature is significantly correlated to lower levels of domestic violence.[37] A New Zealand study showed that every 1 per cent increase in the amount of green space within three kilometres (2 miles) of an individual's home was associated with a 4 per cent lower prevalence of anxiety and mood disorders.[38]

Scientists are only beginning to learn why the great outdoors is so great for us, but some intriguing theories are emerging. We have already discussed the importance of bright light and natural colours, but a more novel theory relates to "earthing." We know that our body and brain constantly have electrical impulses running through them—we measure these all the time in medicine—but it has been suggested that to function optimally we need to be "earthed." The easiest way to do that is to kick off rubber-soled shoes and get around bare footed, garden, and spend time in "ion" rich air such as that which is found near running water—such as rivers and the ocean—or very green spaces—such as rainforests. There is some evidence that "earthing" can reduce chronic pain, improve blood sugar control and even boost immunity.[39]

Scientists are only beginning to learn why the great outdoors is so great for us, but some intriguing theories are emerging.

Another interesting theory relates to air quality. In the 1800s, health authorities in London believed that bad-smelling air—referred to as "miasma"—caused cholera breakouts. While the miasma theory was debunked, there is now growing interest—

and concern—regarding the impact of air quality on people's health and wellbeing. Clearly, poor air quality can trigger respiratory problems, but scientists are discovering that the air we breathe might have other surprising effects too. For example, a study found that people living less than 500 metres (about 1650 feet) above sea level were five times more likely to be obese than those living above 3000 metres (about 10,000 feet).[40] The reason why "thin air" might be "thinning" is that it causes biochemical changes that cause the Limbo to suppress appetite.

But there is more to air than just how thin it is. Other researchers are suggesting that rising carbon dioxide levels in our atmosphere might be contributing to the obesity epidemic as they too can cause biochemical changes in the Limbo resulting in increased appetite.[41] Over the past 50 years, atmospheric carbon dioxide levels have increased by about 40 per cent, while obesity has doubled. So if you now have a sudden interest in breathing less carbon dioxide, you will be interested to learn that the carbon dioxide levels in the air inside sealed rooms can be 20 to 100 times higher than outside![42]

Regardless of the mechanisms, studies consistently show that people who are more connected to nature suffer less anxiety and anger, and enjoy more vitality and happiness.[43] Blue and green should often be seen—and touched and breathed and smelled.

Putting it into action

1. Go and play outside!

Make an effort to get outside while the sun is shining for at least 30 minutes each day. As explained earlier, don't stare into the sun to get your bright light therapy but immerse yourself in naturally lit environments. While you are outside, perform some moderate-intensity physical activity at the same time, so you get a double happiness hit by *Moving dynamically* while *Immersing in an uplifting natural environment*! A study in the United Kingdom found that people who are physically active in natural environments, such as woods and forests, have about half the risk of suffering from poor mental health than those who don't.[44]

2. See a sunrise.

Find a natural environment in which to see a sunrise. Don't stare at it directly, but be there when it happens. Enjoy it. Test and see if the morning light gives you a lift and starts your day right.

Recap

Our Limbo is highly impressed by sights, sounds and smells, and it simply loves those that come from natural environments. Take it to its happy place and it can help you be happy too!

1. G W Kim, J K Song and G W Jeong (2011), "Neuro-anatomical evaluation of human suitability for rural and urban environment by using fMRI," *Korean Journal of Medical Physics*, 22, pages 18–27.

2. A Mantler and A C Logan (2015), "Natural environments and mental health," *Advances in Integrative Medicine*, 2, pages 5–12.

3. T H Kim, G W Jeong, H S Baek, G W Kim, T Sundaram, H K Kang, S W Lee, H J Kim and J K Song (2010), "Human brain activation in response to

visual stimulation and rural urban scenery pictures: A functional magnetic resonance imaging study," *The Science of the Total Environment*, 408, pages 2600–7.

4. L Lottrup, U K Stigsdotter, H Henrik Meilby and A G Claudi (2015), "The workplace window view: A determinant of office workers' work ability and job satisfaction," *Landscape Research*, 40, pages 57–75.

5. J A Benfield, G A Rainbolt, P A Bell and G Donovan (2013), "Classrooms with nature views: Evidence of differing student perceptions and behaviors," *Environment and Behavior*, 47(2), pages 140–57.

6. D Simmons (2011), "Colour and emotion" in C Biggam, C Hough, C Kay and D Simmons (editors), *New Direction in Colour Studies*, John Benjamins Publishing Company.

7. R Mehta and R Zhu (2009), "Blue or Red? Exploring the Effect of Color on Cognitive Task Performances," *Sciencexpress*, February 5, 2009, page 1.

8. ibid.

9. Simmons, op cit.

10. ibid.

11. B Vyssoki, N Praschak-Rieder, G Sonneck, V Blüml, M Willeit, S Kasper and N D Kapusta (2012), "Effects of sunshine on suicide rates," *Comprehensive Psychiatry*, 53, pages 535–39.

12. A Tuunainen, D F Kripke and T Endo (2010), "Light therapy for non-seasonal depression," *Cochrane Database of Systematic Reviews*, 2, Article No: CD004050.

13. R W Lam, A J Levitt, R D Levitan, E E Michalak, R Morehouse, R Ramasubbu, L N Yatham and E M Tam (2016), "Efficacy of Bright Light Treatment, Fluoxetine, and the Combination in Patients With Nonseasonal Major Depressive Disorder: A Randomized Clinical Trial," *Journal of the American Medical Association Psychiatry*, 73(1), pages 56–63.

14. E R Stothard, A W McHill, C M Depner, B R Birks, T M Moehlman, H K Ritchie, J R Guzzetti, E D Chinoy, M K LeBourgeois, J Axelsson and K P Wright (2016), "Circadian Entrainment to the Natural Light-Dark Cycle across Seasons and the Weekend," *Current Biology*, 27, pages 1–6.

15. Lam, et al, op cit; J S Terman, M Terman, E Lo and T B Cooper (2001), "Circadian time morning light administration and therapeutic response in winter depression," *Archives of General Psychiatry*, 58, pages 69–75.

16. Mantler and Logan, op cit.

17. G Vandewalle, S Schwartz, D Grandjean, C Wuillaume, E Balteau, C Degueldre, M Schabus, C Phillips, A Luxen, D J Dijk and P Maquet (2010), "Spectral quality of light modulates emotional brain responses in humans," *Proceedings of the National Academy of Sciences of the United States of America*, 107, pages 19549–54.

18. Tuunainen, et al, op cit.

19. M L Chanda and D J Levitin (2013), "The neurochemistry of music," *Trends in Cognitive Sciences*, 17(4), pages 179–93.

20. Y L Ferguson and K M Sheldon (2013), "Trying to Be Happier Really Can Work: Two Experimental Studies," *Journal of Positive Psychology*, 8, pages 23–33.

21. C Brewer, "Music and learning: Integrating music into the classroom," John Hopkins School of Education, <archive.education.jhu.edu/PD/newhorizons/strategies/topics/Arts%20in%20Education/brewer.htm>.

22. H Bringman, K Giesecke, A Thorne and S Bringman (2009), "Relaxing music as pre-medication before surgery: A randomised controlled trial," *Acta Anaesthesiologica Scandinavica*, 53(6), pages 759–64.

23. ibid.

24. H Kimata (2003), "Listening to Mozart reduces allergic skin wheal responses and in vitro allergen-specific IgE production in atopic dermatitis patients with latex allergy," *Behavioral Medicine*, 29, pages 1, 15-19.

25. T Babikian, L Zeltzer, R Tachdjian, L Henry, E Javanfard, L Tucci, M Goodarzi and R Tachdijian (2013), "Music as medicine: A review and historical perspective," *Alternative & Complementary Therapies*, 19, pages 251–4.

26. D L Clark, N N Boutros and M F Mendez (2010), *The Brain and Behavior: An Introduction to Behavioral Neuroanatomy* (3rd edition), Cambridge University Press.

27. J LeDoux (1998), *The Emotional Brain*, Phoenix.

28. Mantler and Logan, op cit.

29. E O Wilson (1984), *Biophilia*, Harvard University Press.

30. E A McMahan and D Estes (2015), "The Effect of Contact With Natural Environments on Positive and Negative Affect: A Meta-Analysis," *The Journal of Positive Psychology*, 10(6), <http://dx.doi.org/10.1080/17439760.2014.994224>.

31. R Louv (2011), *The Nature Principle: Human restoration and the end of nature-deficit disorder*, Algonquin Books.

32. Mantler and Logan, op cit.

33. M Block, D B Stern, K Raman, S Lee, J Carey, A A Humphreys, F Mulhern, B Calder, D Schultz, C N Rudick, A J Blood and H C Breiter (2014), "The relationship between self-report of depression and media usage," *Frontiers in Human Neuroscience*, 8, Article 712, pages 1–10.

34. S Kaplan (1995), "The restorative benefits of nature: Toward an integrative framework," *Journal of Clinical Psychiatry*, 66(10), pages 1254–69.

35. D G Pearson and T Craig (2014), "The great outdoors? Exploring the

mental health benefits of natural environments," *Frontiers in Psychology*, 5(1178), pages 1–4.

36. R S Ulrich (1984), "View Through a Window May Influence Recovery from Surgery," *Science*, 224, pages 420–1.

37. F E Kuo and W C Sullivan (2001), "Aggression and violence in the inner city: Effects of environment via mental fatigue," *Environmental Behavior*, 33(4), pages 543–71.

38. D Nutsford, A L Pearson and S Kingham (2013), "An ecological study investigating the association between access to urban green space and mental health," *Public Health*, 127, pages 1005–11.

39. J Oschman (2011), "Chronic disease: Are we missing something?" *Journal of Alternative and Complementary Medicine*, 17(4), pages 283-285.

40. J D Voss, P Masuoka, B J Webberm A I Scher and R L Atkinson (2013), "Association of elevation, urbanization and ambient temperature with obesity prevalence in the United States," *International Journal of Obesity*, 37, pages 1407–12.

41. L-G Hersoug, A Sjodin and A Astrup (2012), "A proposed potential role for increasing atmospheric CO2 as a promoter of weight gain and obesity," *Nutrition and Diabetes*, 2(3), page e31.

42. ibid.

43. Mantler and Logan, op cit.

44. R Mitchell (2013), "Is physical activity in natural environments better for mental health than physical activity in other environments?" *Social Science & Medicine*, 91, pages 130–4.

S·M·I·L·E·R·S

IMMERSE IN AN UPLIFTING PHYSICAL ENVIRONMENT

Chapter 5

Together feels better

—Immerse in an uplifting *social* environment—

Of all the means procured by wisdom to ensure happiness throughout the whole of life, by far the most important is the acquisition of friends.—Epicurus

Some people bring happiness wherever they go; others bring happiness whenever they go.—Oscar Wilde

Most of us know the feeling. Someone in the group yawns—and then the rest of us are doing it as well. For some people, just mentioning yawning is enough to get them pulling funny faces. For others, seeing a photo of someone yawning is enough to set them off. Researchers report that about half of all adults yawn when they see someone else do it.[1]

And, if you're yawning now—after reading this opening paragraph—you know exactly what I'm talking about.

To better understand why yawning is so socially

contagious, researchers placed people in a MRI (brain scanning) machine to examine what happens in their brains when they observed video of someone else yawning. The researchers discovered that the people's Limbos—their feeling centre—lit up when viewing a yawn.[2] It is now believed that yawning is an expression of empathy—our Limbo is "feeling" the experience of the yawner!

But it is not only the sight of someone yawning that can cause our Limbo to empathetically light up. Scientists have discovered that within our brain are nerves that fire in concert with other people's brain activity. These nerves—referred to as "mirror neurons"—activate in such a way that it is like we are performing and experiencing the actions and emotions that we observe in others.[3] It is believed that mirror neurons help us learn new skills through imitation and help us identify with the feelings of others by empathising with them.[4]

Have you noticed that when someone smiles at you there is a natural tendency to smile back? This is our mirror neurons in our Limbo at work.[5] Or watch someone else bite into a lemon and notice what happens to your salivary glands. More comically, have you ever noticed that when an adult feeds a baby with a spoon they tend to open their mouth as the baby does? It can be hilarious.

Studies have shown that our mirror neurons can even pick up on the subtle things that others do and cause us to imitate them, without us being consciously aware of it. In one experiment, two people were put in a room and given a task that required them to concentrate.[6] Unbeknown to one of the individuals— the "subject"—the other person in the room was really there to influence them. While head-down doing the task, the influencer repeatedly rubbed their face. After a short time, the

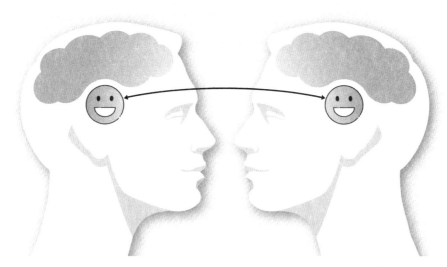

unsuspecting subject began to unconsciously rub their face too. Next, the influencer began to repeatedly move their foot. The subject began to unknowingly do likewise.

Our tendency to mimic each other has been labelled the *Chameleon effect*. It can be so powerful that it has even been suggested that couples can come to look more alike as they mirror each other's facial expressions, resulting in their faces sculpting to appear more similar.[7] As if growing to look more like our pet isn't bad enough, now they tell us that we grow to look more like each other!

Neuroscientists have discovered that, because mirror neurons interact closely with our Limbo, they play a role in how we feel toward others.[8] For example, studies have shown that people who connect well with and feel strongly for others—having a good ability to empathise—tend to demonstrate more "Chameleon" behaviours, meaning they more naturally mimic the actions of those they are empathising with.[9] And people like people who can empathise with them.[10] Indeed, the ability to feel for and with others is considered one of the pillars of emotional intelligence, which is now recognised as far more important than academic intelligence in determining life success.[11] Interestingly, damage to an individual's Limbo, in the form of a stroke or tumour, can result in an inability for them to read how someone is feeling by observing their facial gestures.[12]

It seems our Limbos communicate with each other in their own secret language, in ways that we are not even consciously aware of. For example, have you ever interacted with someone and walked away *feeling* that something wasn't quite right, but you couldn't quite put your finger on why you felt that way? In other words, our Limbo read the situation a certain way but our Leader—our thinking brain—had no idea why, because it was busy thinking about the conversation. In this regard, we need to heed our Limbo more than we do. It is important to ask someone if they are OK when our Limbo gives us the feeling that they might not be.

Note: For those who are spiritually inclined, it is my belief that our Limbo plays an important role in spiritual connection. Unlike our Leader that wants to have everything figured out—it is our thinking brain after all!—the intuitive Limbo is more receptive and open to things that are beyond our comprehension. It is interesting that when people talk about spirituality they use "feeling" language—like "I *felt* impressed" or "I *feel* a deep sense of connection."

How our Limbo tunes in to another's Limbo is not well understood, although eye contact probably plays an important part, not surprising given what we learned in the previous chapter about how the eyes send messages to the Limbo. Some of the studies on eye contact are fascinating. For example, did you know that you are more likely to eat a certain breakfast cereal if the cartoon character on the front of the box is looking you in the eye?[13]

Smell might also play a larger part than we realise in how we connect with each other. Even though we can't smell as well as some animals, such as dogs, our sense of smell still operates in profound ways. Some time ago, researchers discovered that women rated the smell of men—in the form of a T-shirt that had been worn for two nights—as more appealing if the men had an immune system that was different from their own.[14] In effect, the women were subconsciously dialling in to the men through their natural body odour, which is related to their immune system.

Regardless of how our Limbos communicate, we are undeniably wired to connect with others through feelings. The people we are most connected to are those with and for whom we *feel* the strongest. *Feelings connect us.* And we need to be connected to others to be emotionally well.

> The combined results of more than 100 studies show that strong social relationships are as important to a long life as not smoking.

Lack of connection to others—loneliness—is a tremendous source of unhappiness and poor health.[15] The combined results of more than 100 studies show that strong social relationships are as important to a long life as not smoking.[16] A recent study that examined people's brain activity using MRI scans has even shown that when people experience rejection—emotional disconnection—their brain lights up in the same way it does when they experience actual physical pain.[17] Our feelings really can be hurt!

We assimilate when we associate

A few years ago, I ran a marathon. It remains the longest 2 hours, 52 minutes and 47 seconds of my life! I enjoyed the first 30 kilometres (19 miles), but I wanted someone to carry me the final 12 kilometres (7 miles). At one point during the event, when the going started to get tough, I teamed up with two other runners and the three of us took turns leading our little group. I discovered that how I felt was influenced by the runner I was running behind.

We never introduced ourselves but when I ran behind one of my comrades—we'll call him Bouncy Bill—I began to feel strong and that I could go the distance. When the lead switched and I ran behind the other runner—we will call him Awkward Arthur—I began to feel like my legs were going to fall off.

After a few lead changes, I began to notice that the first runner had a springy running style and a rhythmic breathing pattern. When I was behind him, I noticed I began to run in time with him and breathe more easily.

The second runner had an awkward stride and panted like he was blowing out candles. Whenever he took the lead, I began to replicate his untimely gait and my breathing would become erratic. As soon as it dawned on me what was occurring, I became more disciplined in tuning in to Bouncy Bill and tuning out Awkward Arthur.

We tend to assimilate with those with whom we associate. Parents know this reality and spend many nights worrying about the friends their children choose. But few of us are aware of how pervasive and profound the effects of our social ties are. Harvard researchers tracked nearly 5000 people from the town of Framingham for 20 years and examined their social connectedness, and how it affected their happiness and

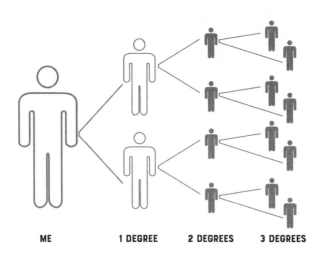

ME   1 DEGREE   2 DEGREES   3 DEGREES

unhappiness.[18] Sophisticated analysis showed that clusters of happiness and unhappiness existed within the social network. But their research discovered that these clusters were not just due to happy people attracting happy people and sad people attracting other sad ones. Over the 20 years of the study, some people became happier and others less so, and the researchers were able to see how happiness—or lack thereof—spread.

Amazingly, the researchers discovered that a change in the happiness of a person in the social network affected the happiness of the friends of their friends' friends! In other words, happiness— and unhappiness—can be infectiously spread up to three degrees of separation. In short, how we feel is socially contagious! Sadly, studies also show that suicide is socially contagious.[19]

We influence each other in such far-reaching ways that it is hardly surprising that researchers keep coming back to relationships as a cornerstone of a life that flourishes.[20] When researchers study the top 10 per cent of happy people, the single most important factor that emerges is that these very happy people have good social relationships.[21]

Renowned happiness researcher and co-author—with his father, Ed Diener—of the book *Happiness: Unlocking the Mysteries of Psychological Wealth*, Dr Robert Biswas-Diener tells an excellent anecdote to sum up the key message. While living for a period with the Kalahari Bushmen to study what made them happy, he went on a hunt with the men. After a long day in the blistering sun and heat of the African desert, the hunting party had nothing to show for their efforts. Yet when they turned to head back to camp they began to sing together—not a forlorn tune, but an upbeat one. Intrigued, Robert quizzed one of the bushmen: "You seem happy, even though we didn't catch anything." The bushman was somewhat puzzled by the question, but replied, "We did not catch anything, but we did not catch anything *together*."[22]

We are designed to operate in community. We are better together. We need each other to do our best and be our best: "The belief that one is cared for, loved, esteemed and valued has been recognised as one of the most (if not the most) influential determinants of wellbeing for people of all ages and cultures."[23]

Relationships are foundational to happiness. That is, of course, if our relationships are positive. And therein lies the problem—not all of them are. And when they are bad, it can be very bad indeed. Essentially, *relationships magnify emotions*—they leverage our Limbo. This is why we can reach higher heights with others, but we can also sink to deeper depths. Thinking about our highest highs and lowest lows, we will probably find that others helped us get there. Indeed, the people who make us most happy also have the ability to make us the most sad.

So how can we discover better relationships so we can *immerse ourselves in an uplifting social environment*? The solution is simple, at least in theory. Let's look at two strategies.

1. Make new friends, the old-school way.

Can you remember anxiously heading off for the first day of school, hoping you would find some friends? And what relief when you were fortunate enough to find some good ones—your Limbo rejoiced and made you feel happy indeed!

The first strategy that can help us immerse ourselves in an uplifting social environment is to make new positive friends. Of course, making friends comes easier to some than others, but the advice our mothers probably gave us on day one of school still rings true: "Show yourself friendly."

Also, go to places where you will find friendly people. A great place to look is where people with a positive orientation gather, such as community interest groups like the local fire brigade or Rotary club, church groups and sporting clubs. So if we are in need of some new uplifting and supportive friends, we should put on our brave face and get out there!

> *A good litmus test to know if you have a supportive network is if you have friends you could call at 3 am if you needed to.*

Professor Martin Seligman says that a good litmus test to know if you have a supportive network is if you have friends you could call at 3 am if you needed to.

Notice that I have advised you to approach this in the "old-school" way. Today, making a new friend often equates to posting a "friend request" on Facebook. A number of studies are indicating that this is not the best way to give our Limbo a lift—it craves "real" as compared to "virtual" connection.

A recent study found that the extent to which young people interacted on Facebook actually predicated a decline in their happiness.[24] Face-to-face interactions did not cause any such decline.

In another study, regular Facebook users were asked to not "show their face on the book" for one month.[25] After one week, participants reported higher levels of life satisfaction and, remarkably, an increase in their social activity and satisfaction with their social life. At the end of the month, they reported feeling happier and less lonely than a comparison group, who continued using the social media site. It was concluded that "social media is a non-stop great news channel—a constant flow of edited lives which distorts our perception of reality." We become dissatisfied with our lives because they don't seem to measure up to the unreal ones we are bombarded by.

Our obsession with social media is often fuelled by a condition referred to as "FoMO"—"Fear of Missing Out." FoMO is defined as a "pervasive apprehension that others might be having rewarding experiences from which one is absent" and is "characterised by the desire to stay continually connected with what others are doing."[26] The Australian Psychological Society states that FoMO affects about 1 in 4 adults and 1 in 2 teens.[27]

I am not suggesting that social media does not have some positive attributes, but the gold standard is—and always will be—to be in the real, rather than virtual, presence of others. As much as you are able, make new friends the old-school way!

2. Strengthen your existing relationships.

It is great to make new relationships, but it can be greater still to strengthen our existing ones. When relationships get hard—and they do—there is a tendency to think that if the other person would just change their attitudes and actions, things would be so much better. Perhaps they would—but good luck with that.

Ultimately, we have little control over others. The only things we really have control over are our *own* attitudes and actions. We can only change our self, and this can sometimes lead to change in others. In fact, sometimes changing ourselves offers the *only* hope for seeing change in others.

Here is where it gets really challenging. If we are committed to strengthening our existing relationships, there are two things we can do to help. But before we consider them, let me stress the need to value and nurture our existing relationships. Life gets so busy that our time is consumed by the *urgent* to the detriment of the *important*. It is too easy to relegate investing time in our relationships, but time is what they require to be healthy and rewarding.

> It is too easy to relegate investing time in our relationships, but time is what they require to be healthy and rewarding.

It is tragic that roughly half of marriages now end in divorce—the *wedding ring* turns into a *suffering* and the *ideal* turns into an *ordeal*. When it does, it can be tempting to imagine that the grass would be greener somewhere else. There are times when relationships should and need to end—in abusive situations, for example—but the ideal is to strengthen the ones you have. So how can this be done?

Love first

We can *love first*. I know it sounds trite, clichéd and cheesy, but love can potentially overcome anything and everything. There are many stories that demonstrate this to be true.

So what does love look like? And what does it mean to *love first*?

I can think of no better way to describe it than in the words of the great love chapter, probably read at more weddings than not: "Love is patient, love is kind. It does not envy, it does not boast, it is not proud. It does not dishonour others, it is not self-seeking, it is not easily angered, it keeps no record of wrongs."[28]

This passage doesn't describe feelings of infatuation or erotic desire, which is often what love is mistakenly portrayed to be. Instead, this love chapter describes selfless actions and attitudes that go against the grain of what comes naturally to most of us.

Read the text again as you think about your current relationships and ask yourself, "Do I do that?" Of course, none of us do it perfectly. But striving to do so has the potential to change the attitudes and actions of others, when nothing else can. To nurture relationships, drawing works better than dragging, and this leads to the call to love first.

Dr Gary Chapman, author of the classic *The 5 Love Languages,* provides excellent insights into how we can intentionally *love first*. He explains that people receive love and feel cared for in different ways—they speak different "love languages." The five love languages are: words of affirmation, receiving gifts, quality time, physical touch and acts of service.[29] Dr Chapman explains that in order for people to feel truly cared for and loved, we need to speak their love language.

Once again, think about the people who are close to you. What might be their love language, bearing in mind that we tend to give the way we would like to receive?[30] Understanding the love language of others, then "speaking" it intentionally, regularly and persistently, can strengthen our existing relationships and, in some instances, even save dying ones.

There is something else we can also do, but we are venturing into challenging territory now.

WORDS OF AFFIRMATION
RECEIVING GIFTS
QUALITY TIME
PHYSICAL TOUCH
ACTS OF SERVICE

Forgive

A psychologist friend of mine who I admire greatly, Dr Dick Tibbits, has written a book titled *Forgive to Live* and developed an associated program.[31] Dr Tibbits makes the point that "everyone has a grievance story, yours may be killing you." Unforgiveness destroys relationships. Dr Tibbits provides some compelling insights into what forgiveness is—and is not—why we should practice it and how to go about it. He has countless stories of people who have finally been able to move forward by putting the past behind them.

Dr Tibbits addresses many misconceptions about forgiveness. Forgiving is not forgetting; it does not wipe our memory. As we learned in Chapter 1, our Limbo is actually designed to remember things that make us feel strongly.

Forgiveness also does not excuse or endorse the actions of others and imply it was or is OK. And it does not negate the consequences of the wrong—perpetrators need not, and often should not, be excused from the consequences of their actions. So what is forgiveness?

Dr Tibbits explains forgiveness as "giving up my right to hurt you for hurting me." Essentially, forgiveness is a circuit breaker of the vicious cycle that unforgiveness creates. It is consciously choosing to move *ourselves* from a negative place of revenge to a positive place of freedom. Interestingly, forgiveness does not even necessarily involve communicating with the person we are forgiving or them requesting to be forgiven. Rather, it is a conscious decision that we make to put the past behind us, and move forward more positively and constructively.

The story is told of two former prisoners of war. One asked the other, "Have you forgiven your captors?" The other man replied, "Never, I will never forgive them." To which came the response, "Then they still hold you captive." It is so hard to do, but forgiveness liberates the forgiver.

While there are incredible and inspiring stories of people who have been able to move on from unimaginable wrong and hurt, lack of forgiveness affects us all. An unwillingness to forgive relatively "small" things can lead to cycles of unforgiveness that ravage relationships. Hurt people hurt people.

Often unforgiveness abounds not so much for a malicious act but for unmet expectations. We think to ourselves, "They should have done this" or "They should know" or "They should have met my needs—and they didn't." We live in a world of high expectations. The media has a lot to answer for as it portrays an unrealistic picture of what our lives should look like. We can find ourselves resenting those—especially those closest to us—who seem to be getting in the way of the perfect life we feel entitled to.

Finally, sometimes the person we need to forgive is our self. Sometimes we need to stop hurting ourselves for the hurt we have caused. While we cannot change the past, we can change the future. If this resonates with you, I would encourage you to consult Dr Tibbits' work to help you move on to a more positive place.

> **Note:** If the past is holding you captive, you might benefit from the book and program called *Forgive to Live* by Dr Dick Tibbits.

There are two key things we can do to strengthen our existing relationships: *love first* and *forgive*. Neither of them are easy. Neither of them come naturally to most of us. But they are things we can do—and they can bring profound positive change. You might be thinking, "Why should I be the one to *love first* and *forgive*?" The short answer is, because ultimately it is for *you*. It can lift *you* and empower *you* to live more.

Putting it into action

1. Love first.
Do something intentional to show someone in your social network that you care for them. Give thought to what might be their "love language"—words of affirmation, receiving gifts, quality time, physical touch or acts of service—then act on that. Take note of how they respond and how it makes you feel.

2. Find a friend.
Do you need to expand your friendship circle? Put your brave face on and go to where friendly people hang out. Make a new friend, the old-school way!

3. Forgive a friend.

Is there someone in your social network you need to forgive? Decide to put the past behind you and move into a more positive place by no longer intentionally hurting them for hurting you.

Recap

Happiness is contagious because our Limbos have a language of their own that connects us with each other. To give our Limbo a lift, we need to immerse ourselves in an uplifting *social* environment because *together feels better*! Make new friends the old-school way and strengthen your existing relationships by taking charge of what *you* can do, which is to love first and forgive.

1. S M Platek, F B Mohamed and G G Gallup (2005), "Contagious yawning and the brain," *Cognitive Brain Research*, 23, pages 448–52.

2. ibid.

3. M Iacoboni (2009), "Imitation, Empathy, and Mirror Neurons," *Annual Review of Psychology*, 60, pages 653–70.

4. J A Bastiaansen, M Thioux and C Keysers (2009), "Evidence for mirror systems in emotions," *Philosophical Transactions of the Royal Society B*, 364, pages 2391–404.

5. B Wild, M Erb, M Bartels and W Grodd (2009), "Why are smiles contagious? An fMRI study of the interaction between perception of facial affect and facial movements," *Psychiatry Research: Neuroimaging*, 123, pages 17–36.

6. T L Chartrand and J A Bargh (1999), "The chameleon effect: The perception–behavior link and social interaction," *Journal of Personality and Social Psychology*, 76, pages 893–910.

7. C E Rusbult, E J Finkel, and M Kumashiro (2009), "The Michelangelo phenomenon," *Current Directions in Psychological Science*, 18, pages 305–9.

8. Iacoboni, op cit.

9. Chartrand and Bargh, op cit.

10. ibid.

11. D Goleman (1995), *Emotional Intelligence—Why it can matter more than IQ*, Bloomsbury.

12. J V Haxby, E A Hoffman and M I Gobbini (2002), "Human Neural Systems for Face Recognition and Social Communication," *Biological Psychiatry*, 51, pages 59–67.

13. A Musicus, A Tal and B Wansink (2015), "Eyes in the Aisles: Why Is Cap'n Crunch Looking Down at My Child?" *Environment and Behavior*, 47(7), pages 715–33.

14. C Wedekind, T Seebeck, F Bettens and A J Paepke (1995), "MHC-Dependent mate preferences in humans," *Biological Sciences*, 260(1359), pages 245–9.

15. J Holt-Lunstad, T B Smith and J B Layton (2010), "Social Relationships and Mortality Risk: A Meta-analytic Review," *PLoS Medicine*, 7(7), e1000316; D Ornish (1998), *Love and Survival*, William Morrow.

16. Holt-Lunstad, et al, op cit.

17. E Kross, M G Bermana, W Mischelb, E E Smith and T D Wager (2011), "Social rejection shares somatosensory representations with physical pain," *Proceedings of the National Academy of Science*, 108(15), pages 6270–5.

18. J H Fowler and N A Christakis (2008), "Dynamic spread of happiness in a large social network: Longitudinal analysis over 20 years in the Framingham Heart Study," *British Medical Journal*, 337, a2338.

19. A L Pitman, D P Osborn, K Rantell and M B King (2016), "Bereavement by suicide as a risk factor for suicide attempt: A cross-sectional national UK-wide study of 3432 young bereaved adults," *British Medical Journal Open*, 6, e009948.

20. M Seligman (2011), *Flourish*, Random House.

21. M Seligman (2002), *Authentic Happiness*, Random House.

22. E Diener and R Biswas-Diener (2008), *Happiness: Unlocking the Mysteries of Psychological Wealth*, Blackwell Publishing.

23. H Reis and S Gable (2003), "Toward a positive psychology of relationships" in C Keyes and J Haidt (editors), *Flourishing: Positive psychology and the life well lived*, American Psychological Association.

24. E Kross, P Verduyn, E Demiralp, J Park, D S Lee, N Lin, H Shablack, J Jonides and O Ybarra (2013), "Facebook Use Predicts Declines in

Subjective Well-Being in Young Adults," *PLoS ONE*, 8(8), e69841.

25. Happiness Research Institute (2016), "The Facebook Experiment. Does social media affect the quality of our lives?" <www.happinessresearchinstitute.com>.

26. A K Przybylski, K Murayama, C R DeHaan and V Gladwell (2013), "Motivational, emotional, and behavioural correlates of fear of missing out," *Computers in Human Behavior*, 29, pages 1814–48.

27. Australian Psychological Society (2015), "Stress and wellbeing. How Australians are coping with life," *Australian Psychological Society Stress and Wellbeing Survey 2015*, <www.psychology.org.au/Assets/Files/PW15-SR.pdf>.

28. 1 Corinthians 13:4, 5.

29. G Chapman (2010), *The 5 Love Languages: The Secret to Love that Lasts*, Northfield Publishing.

30. To discover your own love language, and that of others, visit <www.5lovelanguages.com/profile/>.

31. D Tibbits (2016), *Forgive to Live. How forgiveness can save your life* (10th Anniversary Edition), Florida Hospital Publishing.

S·M·I·L·E·R·S

IMMERSE IN AN UPLIFTING SOCIAL ENVIRONMENT

Chapter 6

Feelings follow our focus

−Look to the positive−

When you think things are bad, when you feel sour and blue,
when you start to get mad, you should do what I do!
Just tell yourself, Duckie, you're really quite lucky!
—Dr Seuss

If anything is excellent or praiseworthy—think on such things.
—Philippians 4:8

We have learned about the Limbo—our feeling brain—and we have learned about the Leader—our thinking brain. But let me give you an insight into how my crazy Limbo and Leader can be a bad influence on each other.

Not long after my wife and I were married—before kids came along—I was wandering past the television when a particular image caught my eye. The image was that of worms, those nasty gastrointestinal parasites. I had no interest in the television show—even less after seeing that image—so kept on about my business. But the image stuck.

That night, as I closed my eyes to go to sleep, it was like a big screen had been erected on the back of my eyelids. The image just wouldn't go away and my Leader couldn't stop *thinking* about it. But then things got worse. My Limbo got in on the act and I started to *feel* a bit queasy in my belly. Before long, my Leader *thought* I had worms and my Limbo *felt* like I did.

My wife enjoyed doing the shopping, so I asked her to buy some worming tablets next time she went. Being a loving wife, she replied, "If you want worming tablets, buy them yourself!"

Since there was no way I was going to march into a shop and ask for worming tablets, I tried to give up on the idea, but I couldn't stop *thinking* and *feeling* that something needed to be done. Finally, I could take it no longer.

I knew the local shop sold worming tablets but the *thought* that I might know someone there made me *feel* uneasy, so I drove to the next town. As I walked in, there was a long counter at which a woman was serving several people. I took my place at the far end of the counter. When at last the woman asked if she could help me, I found myself talking very softly so she was drawn toward me and away from the crowd.

I was meaning to say, "Could I please have some worming tablets?" But as I was about to articulate the words, I found myself *thinking* that if I were to say that the woman would surmise that I had worms—and that made me *feel* embarrassed. So I found myself saying, "Could I please get a family worming kit?" I don't even know what that means—you need a *kit* for it?—but it made it sound like it wasn't really for me, that I was just caring for the gastrointestinal wellbeing of my "family."

The woman seemed a little puzzled. Clearly she had never heard it referred to as a "kit" either, but she got the idea enough to ask, "OK, how many in your family?"

It is here that I feel ashamed to continue the story. Of course, I couldn't say "One" as this would have blown my cover and, while "Two" was the correct answer, the *thought* occurred to me that if I did say "Two," the woman would assume there was an even chance that I was the one with the worms.

Feeling somewhat anxious, I found myself answering "Three," hoping that would be the end of it and I could just get out of there!

But that wasn't to be.

"So I can select the right product," she replied, "I have just a couple of questions." I began to squirm. "So when you say three, would that be yourself, wife and child?" she quizzed.

"Yes," I replied sheepishly.

"So how old is your child?"

Now I was *feeling* very anxious and my *thoughts* were running away.

"Four years old," I replied.

A big smile erupted on her face. I was about to learn that she really liked kids. Out of genuine interest, first she wanted to know if it was a girl or a boy. Obviously it was a little girl—I had always wanted to pretend to have a little girl. "And her name?" she asked with delight.

I was impressed with how quickly "Sophie" rolled off my tongue, albeit ashamed at how rapidly I had adapted to this lying business.

To cut a long story short, by the time I exited the shop with my "family worming kit," the woman was looking forward to one day meeting little Sophie, who just loved to wear anything pink and carried a panda teddy around with her everywhere, even on the one day each week that she went to pre-school.

Feelings follow focus

Can you identify with my crazy situation? Have your thoughts and feelings ever spiralled you out of control?

There is a good reason why this happens. Our Limbo is wired to the front portion of our Leader, also known as the frontal cortex.[1] This part of the Leader is responsible for higher-order thinking, for what we give our attention to and focus on. Hence, what we *think* about affects how we *feel*—or to put it succinctly, *feelings follow our focus*.

A good example of this happening is the "Don't go there" topic. You know, those topics that we don't want to be reminded of, or we avoid bringing up with someone, because if we do, things go badly emotionally. In essence, the Leader conjures negative thoughts and the Limbo follows.

A man was once telling me how he parked his boat out the front of his house with a "For sale" sign on it but, during the night, someone took a liking to it, hitched it to their car and simply drove away. As he retold the story, which had happened many years earlier, I could see the steam starting to rise.

Feelings follow our focus. We can hurt our own feelings by what we think about and focus on. As the stoic Roman philosopher Seneca once said, "A man is as miserable as he *thinks* he is."

Fortunately, it works positively as well. Ask a new grandparent about their grandchild—if you have plenty of time!—and watch their spirits lift. Again, *feelings follow our focus.* Sometimes when I give presentations to a group, I ask the audience to share uplifting stories—life's wins and successes—and invariably the mood in the room lifts.

But not only does our focus feed our feelings, our feelings also feed our focus. While the front portion of our Leader is wired to and sends messages to our Limbo, our Limbo sends messages back. This is why we can enter upward and downward spirals in our thoughts and feelings. I refer to them as "Limbo loops."[2] The Leader and Limbo can spur each other on.

Consider the following example of a downward Limbo loop. It starts when we hear about a house that has been robbed and our Leader starts to *think* about it. These thoughts arrive at our

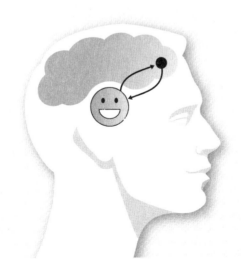

two-year-old-like Limbo, which causes it to initiate a *feeling* of mild anxiousness. Those anxious feelings feed back to the Leader, which causes it to focus more intently on the topic and begin to imagine where someone would break in to our house. Our Limbo becomes even more distressed by the thought of our house being broken into and dials up our anxiety level.

The Leader is really primed now and begins to imagine scenes of someone levering open our window and snooping around in our room. Our Limbo is terrified by this thought and, that night, we lie in bed in a cold sweat, rocking in the foetal position and sucking our thumb with the covers over our head for protection. A single thought snowballed into an intense feeling as the Leader and Limbo dragged each other down.

But the same can be seen for upward Limbo loops. It starts when someone compliments us on how we look. Instantly, our Leader paints a mental picture of us looking like a super model—and our Limbo likes it! Our Limbo passes the good feeling back to the Leader, which in turn starts to notice other good things as well.

Before we know it, the Limbo and the Leader are bouncing off each other with positive thoughts creating positive feelings creating more positive thoughts. We are on an upward spiral! Psychologists refer to it as the "broaden-and-build" theory of positive emotions as it leads to "expansion"—expansion of our

> **Note:** The Limbo loop might explain the experience of *déjà vu*.[3] In recycling information from our Limbo to our Leader, our Leader thinks the Limbo is dredging up a memory. As a consequence, we are overcome with the feeling, "I have been here before."

mindset, our openness to social situations and essentially a greater joy of living.[4]

Limbo loops mean that *thoughts and feelings breed their own kind, good or bad.* So how can we arrest downward Limbo loops and activate upward ones instead?

Choosing the loops

Have you ever heard it said to someone who is emotionally down, "Stop feeling that way" or "Just pick yourself up"? Perhaps someone has said it to you. Such advice is about as helpful as saying to someone with a broken leg, "Just walk it off!" How we feel comes from our "two-year-old" Limbo—try telling a two-year-old to stop throwing a tantrum and see how effective it is! We can't expect our Limbo to just shake off a feeling, but what we can do is use the frontal cortex of our Leader to influence it in the direction we want it to go. We can do that by choosing what to think about.

Regarded by some as the father of American psychology, Dr William James once said, "Our greatest weapon against stress is the ability to choose one thought over another." It is not only stress that this relates to, the same applies to other unwanted feelings—our greatest defence is our ability to choose what we think about.

Sadly, many people don't utilise the great weapon that is their ability to choose their thoughts. In fact, many people don't think at all! Instead, they give their two-year-old-like Limbo the reins. In his book *Emotional Intelligence: Why it matters more than IQ*, Daniel Goleman has a chapter titled "When smart is dumb" in which he recounts stories of very intelligent people—even straight-A students—who do the dumbest things because they let their Limbo take over.[5] It is known as "emotional hijacking,"

87

when the Limbo mutinies against the rightful captain—the Leader—and does whatever it feels like.

There are some gory stories that demonstrate how important the frontal cortex of the Leader is in controlling the Limbo.

One of the classic tales is that of Phineas Gage, who survived a massive head injury caused by a railroad spike blasting through his head, destroying much of his frontal lobe. Before the accident, he had been a polite, upstanding gentleman but afterwards he was a degenerate. With his Leader no longer able to lead, the Limbo did its own thing and his friends all agreed that "he was no longer Gage."[6]

The second unbelievable story relates to a time in our not-too-distant past when it was thought a good idea to destroy the connections between the frontal lobe of the Leader and the Limbo. In the first half of the 20th century, an estimated 40,000 individuals in the United States alone were subjected to the barbaric procedure called a "frontal lobotomy." I won't go into the details of how the procedure was performed or the absurdity of why, but it left those on the receiving end emotionally blunted. Without the ability for their frontal lobe to lead the Limbo, they "lost the remnants of their mental health."[7]

The point is that our Leader is meant to lead. It is meant to take good care of the "two-year-old" Limbo, and it can do this by choosing to *think* in the right way, about the right things. Everyone has heard about the purported benefits of "positive thinking," but now we understand how and why it actually works—we are wired that way!

In fact, new understandings of how our brains work have

highlighted more than ever the importance of being intentional about adopting a positive outlook and *looking to the positive*. Where once it was believed that the brain was quite rigid in its orientation, now we know that the brain has an amazing ability to mould and change itself.[8] The notion of "brain plasticity"—the brain's ability to create and strengthen its connections and pathways—is an exciting frontier of neuroscience research.

However, this understanding presents both an opportunity and a warning. The opportunity is that we can learn new tricks—even old dogs can! We can strengthen the connections between our Leader and Limbo in a positive way, so that we can get better at performing upward Limbo loops. The warning is that we can also improve our ability to perform downward Limbo loops.

> *We can strengthen the connections between our Leader and Limbo in a positive way, so that we can get better at performing upward Limbo loops.*

I teach a class at university called "Skill acquisition" and one concept I drum into my students is that "practice makes permanent." It is not true that "practice makes perfect," only *perfect* practice makes perfect. To live more emotionally up on a more regular basis, we need to perfect and practice the art of thinking positively.

Look to the positive

If you were put in a corner with nothing but your brain to keep you entertained and were given the task of making yourself feel down, how long would it take before you were successful? Thinking negatively comes easily for many of us, perhaps because we have been practising it for many years. Now that we know how

Limbo loops work, it is hardly surprising that repetitive negative thinking, such as worry and ruminating on negative things, makes people more vulnerable to anxiety and depression.[9]

But if we know where to go—in our thinking—to get on a downward Limbo loop, doesn't it make sense that it can work in the opposite direction as well? So how can we stop "stinking thinking"?—to borrow the words of Zig Ziglar, one the most renowned motivational speakers of the 20th century.

The trick for combating negative thinking—and the downward Limbo loops that can ensue—is to replace negative thoughts with positive ones.[10] But this requires us to be intentional. At least a third of our thought flow each day is undirected,[11] which means that if we don't take care to lead it to a positive place we can easily and unwittingly find ourselves in a negative one. Because our Leader doesn't stay idle for long, we can't expect it to stop thinking about negative things without giving it something else to think about—otherwise, it might start thinking about something even worse! So what positive things should we think about?

When it comes to really engaging our Leader in positive thinking, questions are the answer. Questions have the ability to really get the cogs turning in the frontal cortex of our Leader, as they force it to focus. There are three questions in particular

Some places might be better for beating negative thinking than others. A study found that, when people went on a walk through a natural environment, they didn't ruminate as much on negative things as compared to when they walked through an urban environment.[12] This again highlights the benefits of immersing ourselves in green spaces, as we learned about in Chapter 4!

that can direct us toward an upward Limbo loop and they relate to how we *look to the positive* in relation to the past, present and future.

Question 1: What am I truly grateful for?

What are three things you are truly grateful for? Don't just give a trite answer. Pause for a moment, give the question your full attention, and really think about it.

Do the responses come easily or do you struggle? If you were to take the time, how long a list could you compile?

Most of us don't take the time to think regularly about what we are grateful for. This is to our detriment, because expressing gratitude is now known to have many benefits, both mental and physical.[13] While expressing gratitude has been promoted by faith traditions for millennia, it is only in the past decade or so that its ability to lift us emotionally has been scientifically documented.

> *Expressing gratitude is now known to have many benefits, both mental and physical.*

In 2003, researchers from the University of California and Miami conducted several "gratitude experiments" and concluded that consciously focusing on blessings, as compared to burdens, had both emotional and interpersonal benefits.[14] A few years later, other researchers reported that when people participated in a "gratitude visit," which involves writing and delivering a letter of gratitude to someone who had been especially significant to them, the giver's level of happiness increased and remained elevated for one month afterward.[15]

Practising gratitude has now been repeatedly shown to help people of all ages feel more emotionally well, including children,[16] early adolescents,[17] college students,[18] and middle-aged and older adults.[19] Practising gratitude is now one of the most robust strategies used in positive psychology for increasing happiness.[20]

So why is being grateful so uplifting? Dr Martin Seligman explains that gratitude "amplifies good memories about the past,"[21] which puts us in a positive frame of mind. And that positive mindset can help us *look to the positive* in the present and future.

As the old saying goes, "If a fellow isn't thankful for what he's got, he isn't likely to be thankful for what he'll get."

Question 2: What went well today?

In a fascinating study, participants were asked to complete a short writing activity called "Three good things" before they went to sleep every night for one week.[22] The task involved them writing down three things that went well that day and why they went well. The participants benefitted so much from the activity that many of them stuck with it, but what was truly

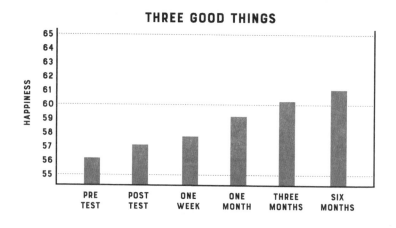

THREE GOOD THINGS

remarkable is that their happiness progressively *increased* for the next six months. Normally in studies like this, we see a "treatment effect," which gradually dwindles to nothing over time, but in this instance the effect gradually grew!

Question 3: What am I looking forward to?

What do you have coming up in the near future that gives you a warm fuzzy every time you think about it? If you are struggling for a good response—and something vague like "the weekend" is inadequate—you had better do something about it.

When we are devoid of something to get excited about—to look forward to—life becomes dull and mundane, and we are unlikely to be filled with the joy of living.

I aim to always have something that I am eagerly anticipating. My wife often comments that the anticipation of an event is often better than the reality of it, but that is OK because it serves us well in the

> *The excitement of looking forward to something can be all it takes to pick us up when we are feeling down.*

period leading up to the event. The excitement of looking forward to something can be all it takes to pick us up when we are feeling down. One of the possible reasons children are, for the most part, upbeat and happy is they have an innate capacity to get excited. A tragedy of ageing is that we are expected to "grow up" and put this behind us. But how good was life when we counted down the number of sleeps until Christmas or our birthday?

So what do you have coming up in the near future that you are looking forward to, even excited about? If you are drawing a blank, remedy it! Go find something to get excited about!

Another way we can look positively to the future is to be hopeful. Hope is having positive expectations about the future and numerous studies show that people with hope are happier, and suffer less depression and stress.[23] So do you have hope?

Dr Victor Frankl was an Austrian neurologist and psychiatrist who narrowly survived the holocaust. As a prisoner in a death camp, he endured unspeakable atrocities, but as a doctor, he found himself caring for—and observing—his fellow prisoners. In his book *Man's Search for Meaning*, he tells of how a disproportionate number of his fellow prisoners died in the week after Christmas, 1944. At first, it seemed inexplicable. There had been no change in work conditions, rations, the weather or anything else that could have added to the hardship they were enduring. After much thought, the "cause of death" became apparent to him—there had been rumours in the camp that the Allies were coming to liberate them and that they would be home by Christmas. With their hopes dashed, the people perished.[24]

Anne Frank was correct when she penned, "Where there is hope, there's life." Hope is literally life-giving.

Hope is one of my favourite words. It makes me happier and is a great source of comfort, especially when things are not going well. As the quote attributed to John Lennon puts it, "Everything will be OK in the end. If it's not OK, it's not the end." That is hope speaking. It is a wonderful expression of looking to the future with positivity.

Putting it into action

1. What went well?

Take 10–15 minutes at the end of each day to think about and write down three things that went well that day and why they went well. You might find that doing this activity shortly before you go to bed will also help you sleep better.[25]

2. Gratitude visit.

Think about someone who has had a significant positive impact on your life and write it down in a few paragraphs. Now the hard part: Share it with the person, ideally face-to-face.

3. Mark it in your diary!

Are you in need of something to look forward to? Mark something in your diary that will give you an eager sense of anticipation every time you think about it.

Recap

It is possible to get on upward and downward spirals in the way that we think and feel, because our Leader and Limbo are connected in a loop-like fashion. We can arrest downward "Limbo loops" by changing what we choose to think about. To live more, we need to *look to the positive* in the past, present and future because *feelings follow our focus*.

1. D L Clark, N N Boutros and M F Mendez (2010), *The Brain and Behavior: An Introduction to Behavioral Neuroanatomy* (3rd edition), Cambridge University Press.

2. E L Garland, B Fredrickson, A M Kring, D P Johnson, P S Meyer and D L Penn (2010), "Upward Spirals of Positive Emotions Counter Downward Spirals of Negativity: Insights from the Broaden-and-Build Theory and Affective Neuroscience on The Treatment of Emotion Dysfunctions and Deficits in Psychopathology," *Clinical Psychology Review*, 30(7), pages 849–64.

3. Clark, et al, op cit.

4. Garland, et al, op cit.

5. D Goleman (1995), *Emotional Intelligence*, Bantam Books.

6. S Twomney (2010), "Phineas Gage: Neuroscientists most famous patient," *Smithsonian Magazine*, January, 2010, <www.smithsonianmag.com/history/phineas-gage-neurosciences-most-famous-patient-11390067/>.

7. Encyclopedia Britannica, "Labotomy surgery," <www.britannica.com/topic/lobotomy>.

8. N Doige (2010), *The Brain that Changes Itself*, Scribe.

9. P M McEvoy, H Watson, E R Watkins and P Nathan (2013), "The relationship between worry, rumination, and comorbidity: Evidence for repetitive negative thinking as a transdiagnostic construct," *Journal of Affective Disorders*, 151, pages 313–20.

10. Garland, et al, op cit; S Nolen-Hoeksema, B E Wisco and S Lyubomirsky (2008), "Rethinking Rumination," *Perspectives on Psychological Science,* 3, page 400.

11. E Klinger and W Cox (1988), "Dimensions of thought flow in everyday life," *Imagination, Cognition and Personality*, 7(2), pages 105-128.

12. G N Bratman, J P Hamilton, K S Hahn, G C Daily and J J Gross (2015), "Nature experience reduces rumination and subgenual prefrontal cortex activation," *Proceedings of the National Academy of Sciences*, 112(28), pages 8567–72.

13. A M Wood, J J Froh and A W A Geraghty (2010), "Gratitude and well-being: A review and theoretical integration," *Clinical Psychology Review,* 30(7), pages 890–905.

14. R A Emmons and M E McCullough (2003), "Counting Blessings Versus Burdens: An Experimental Investigation of Gratitude and Subjective Well-Being in Daily Life," *Journal of Personality and Social Psychology,* 84(2), pages 377–89.

15. M E Seligman, T A Steen, N Park and C Peterson (2005), "Positive Psychology Progress. Empirical Validation of Interventions," *American Psychologist*, 60(5), pages 410–21.

16. J J Froh, T B Kashdan, K M Ozimkowski and N Miller (2009), "Who benefits the most from a gratitude intervention in children and adolescents? Examining positive affect as a moderator," *The Journal of Positive Psychology*, 4(5), pages 408–22.

17. J J Froh, W J Sefick and R A Emmons (2008), "Counting blessings in early adolescents: An experimental study of gratitude and subjective well-being," *Journal of School Psychology*, 46, pages 213–33.

18. K M Sheldon and S Lyubomirsky (2006), "How to increase and sustain positive emotion: The effects of expressing gratitude and visualizing best possible selves," *Journal of Positive Psychology*, 1(2), pages 73–82.

19. Seligman, et al, op cit.

20. ibid.

21. M E Seligman (2002), *Authentic Happiness*, William Heinemann.

22. Seligman, et al (2005), op cit.

23. G M Alarcon, N A Bowling and S Khazon (2013), "Great expectations: A meta-analytic examination of optimism and hope," *Personality and Individual Differences*, 54, pages 821–27.

24. V Frankl (1946), *Man's Search for Meaning*, Beacon Press.

25. Wood, et al, op cit.

S·M·I·L·E·R·S

 **LOOK TO THE POSITIVE**

Chapter 7

Food feeds our mood

—Eat nutritiously—

The pleasure of the second taste of Basset's French vanilla ice cream is less than half of the first, and by the fourth taste, it's just calories.—Martin Seligman

Your state of mind might be dependent upon your state of gut. —John Cryan

In the 1970s, the Lard Information Council proudly issued advertisements espousing the virtues of lard for wellbeing and happiness. (In case you are wondering, lard is processed pig fat.) It is comical today to read the assertions made on the advertising posters. In bold print over a happy young family walking hand in hand on the beach were the words, "They're happy because they eat lard." Plastered above a photo of a sporty girl jogging effortlessly through a field, another caption read, "Lard helps me live life to the full!"

Obviously, some clever marketers recognised that everyone wants to be happy and full of life, so it made sense to link lard to positive living in the interest of selling more lard. The marketing idea is so good that it persists today. For example, McDonald's "McHappy Meal" and Coca Cola's "Open Happiness" campaign attempt to capitalise on it. But while it is clever advertising, it might come as a shock to learn that it is completely unfounded. Lard doesn't give our Limbo a lift.

Food and mood

In this chapter, we will learn about some fascinating recent medical findings that relate to how food can affect our mood and what we can eat to be "up" more. But before we do, let's just back up for a moment and consider an interesting question. Why do we humans get "down" and depressed? We have emotions for a reason. For example, we experience fear because it motivates us for "fight or flight." We experience love because it bonds us and inspires us to self-sacrifice. But why do we experience low mood? What's the use of it? Scientists have come up with a novel answer to this question.[1]

Today, most people die from lifestyle-related diseases, conditions linked to factors such as poor eating patterns, physical inactivity and high levels of stress. But this is unique to our time in history. In all previous generations, people mostly died from bugs, such as a bacteria or virus, that invaded their bodies. You know the story: The plague swept through town and wiped out every third person.

Our body has an incredibly sophisticated inbuilt line of defence for dealing with foreign invaders such as these "bugs"— our immune system. But while our immune system is doing its thing—fighting off foreign invaders—it needs us to do two things to help it. First, it needs us to conserve energy because raging battles with foreign invaders is energy-demanding, so our body needs to redirect as much energy as it can toward this important task. Next, it needs us to stay away from other people to prevent the bugs spreading and making the situation worse.

Have you noticed that this is exactly what happens when we have the flu? We feel lethargic and there is a tendency to socially isolate ourselves.

In effect, we are displaying the symptoms of depression. Scientists have hypothesised that our brain may create a "low mood" as a natural way to help our body best deal with foreign invaders.[2]

While these depressive symptoms—low mood and feeling antisocial—might be helpful in the short-term as we fight off bugs that come and go, feeling like this in the long-term is not helpful at all. But could this idea of depression being a response to foreign invaders help explain why so many people are depressed today? The answer might be yes—and it implicates our diet.

In his best-selling book, *In Defense of Food*, Michael Pollan makes the point that most of what we eat today is not "food" as far as the body is concerned. Instead, it is a "food-like substance."[3] Food-like substances are processed, don't grow on trees, often come in a package or box, and wouldn't be recognised by your great-great-grandma in her day. And here is the point: Scientists have discovered that, if our great-great-grandma wouldn't recognise it as food, our body doesn't either. Instead, it sees it as a foreign invader and hence goes into defence—and depressed—mode.

Of course, these food-like substances are not as ferocious as other foreign invaders, such as the black plague, but they can still take a massive toll on us because, unlike the black plague— here one day, gone the next—food-like substances just keep coming. Many of us "infect" ourselves with them a number of times every day!

The takeaway message is that the poor excuse for "food" we consume day-in, day-out might be causing us to feel down as our bodies attempt to deal with the unwelcome invasion. So what can be done about it? Thankfully—or sadly, depending on your perspective—the solution isn't to eat more lard, despite what the Lard Information Council might say.

I helped develop and am a key presenter for the Complete Health Improvement Program (CHIP), a nutrition-centred program that helps people with chronic conditions such as heart disease and diabetes to manage and even reverse their ailments. CHIP is now in more than 10 countries around the world with tens of thousands of participants, and the outstanding outcomes of the program have been published in many reputable medical journals.[4] But here is the intriguing thing: While CHIP targets physical ailments, it also lifts people's mood.[5] Only days after starting the program people say that it is as if a "fog lifts" from their brain—we hear that comment so often—and they feel better. So what is it about CHIP that makes this difference?

> *The poor excuse for "food" we consume day-in, day-out might be causing us to feel down as our bodies attempt to deal with the unwelcome invasion.*

CHIP promotes a plant-based diet, dominated by whole fruits, vegetables, grains and legumes. It emphasises foods-as-grown— or "first-order" foods, as I call them. The body recognises these foods as "real food," so welcomes them on board as a friend, not foe. As these foods are not seen as foreign invaders and our

101

body doesn't have to dedicate resources to fighting them, it is not surprising that eating this way results in higher energy levels and a mood lift.

Many studies are now showing a strong connection between plant-based diets and positive mood.[6] In a study involving more than 80,000 people in Great Britain, the researchers discovered a dose-response relationship between the consumption of fruits and vegetables and happiness—the more fruits and vegetables people consumed, the happier they were, even after taking into account a number of other personal, social and economic factors known to influence happiness.[7] Of course, there was a limit to the mood lift—after about eight serves of fruits and vegetables a day the happiness benefits plateaued off.

However, this study only looked at associations, so the researchers couldn't tell if eating more fruits and vegetables increased happiness or whether happy people just tend to eat more fruit and vegetables. What is the cause and what is the effect?

To test this, researchers from New Zealand tracked people's fruit and vegetable consumption and happiness for several weeks.[8] Again, they found that people who ate the most fruit and vegetables were the happiest, with about eight total serves daily being ideal. But, more importantly, they also observed a causal effect whereby the participants reported feeling happier *the day after* they consumed higher levels of fruits and vegetables.

Another study by Australian researchers found that a Mediterranean-style diet, which emphasised fruits, vegetables, grains and legumes, relieved depression four times more effectively than when only social support was offered to the study participants.[9] More recently, studies have found that a higher consumption of fruit and vegetables not only improves happiness, but also other mental measures including curiosity and creativity.[10] Berries can beat the blues and carrots can cultivate creativity!

Plant-based diets certainly seem to be the pick for improving mood. In one study, the researchers took omnivores—people who eat meat and plant foods—and randomly assigned them to three groups.[11] The first group kept eating what they always ate. The second group was instructed to eat no meat except plenty of fish containing omega-3 fatty acids, which have been linked to mental health—although this has been challenged recently.[12] The third group was placed on a plant-based—vegetarian—diet. After only two weeks, those who had adopted the plant-based diet recorded a significant improvement in their mood, while the other groups had no change.

So why can choosing a plant slant to our diet give our Limbo a lift? It turns out there are many reasons, but it is here that we enter the problem I have with nutrition research—it gets finicky and complex. Nutrition researchers are always trying to drill down to the fine details of what particular nutrient in a particular food has a particular effect. It seems it is not enough to know

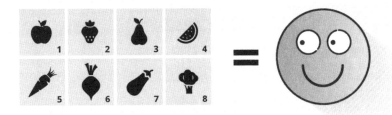

that blueberries are really good for us; nutrition researchers want to know what particular ingredient in blueberries—of the thousands they contain—is the *one thing* that does the good.

But scientists are slowly coming to the realisation that there is no *one thing*, there are *many* things! Blueberries are so health-giving because of the myriad of things they contain and how those myriad of things interact and work together. Note that I'm only using blueberries as an example—other plant foods are just as nutritious! Studies have consistently shown that if you isolate a particular vitamin or nutrient thought to be some kind of "magic bullet," then give it as a supplement to people in isolation, it usually isn't helpful at all and, in some cases, is actually harmful! What researchers are realising is that "whole foods" are the way to go.[13]

Of course, I understand that some people like to drill down to the nitty-gritty. If you are one of them, here are some of the reasons it is thought plant-based diets can be mood lifters: they are low in arachidonic acid, high in folate, have anti-inflammatory properties, are rich in antioxidants—and there are literally hundreds of these—contain human neurotransmitters such as serotonin, and promote better glycaemic control.[14] Do you feel better for knowing that?

Personally, I like to keep it simple, so I would like to offer one simple approach to eating nutritiously for feeling great. But before I do, let me share one of the most fascinating areas of current medical research that will highlight why the approach I offer works wonders for our Limbo.

The biggest part of you

If I were to ask what is the biggest part of our body, how would you respond? Males might say their muscles. Wrong—

even if you are a professional body builder. Your skin perhaps? We certainly do have a lot of it—more than we need, it seems, as we grow older—but still wrong. The biggest part of us is actually our gut. I know that fact is not exactly conducive to a healthy self-esteem, but let me explain.

"Gut" is not actually a slang term—there is a medical journal that even goes by that name!

Our gut—or "gastrointestinal tract"—is more than 9 metres (30 feet) long and its inside lining has a surface area 20 to 100 times greater than our skin. But here is the truly outstanding part: We have at least 100 trillion bacteria in our gut, roughly 10 times more than the number of "human" cells we have in our entire body![15] I hate to break the news to you, but you are more bacteria than human.

> It is now known that the health of our gut and its bacteria has a profound effect on our overall health and wellbeing.

The study of these bacteria is one of the most intriguing frontiers of medical research. It is now known that the health of our gut and its bacteria has a profound effect on our overall health and wellbeing. One of the reasons for this is that more than 70 per cent of our immune system is distributed around our gut[16]—obviously there are a lot of nasties that pass through our gastrointestinal tract that our body needs to defend itself against. So it is not surprising to learn that the health of an individual's gut bacteria is now linked to numerous conditions including allergies, diabetes, Crohn's disease, certain cancers and even autism.[17]

Our gut bacteria are now known to affect our predisposition

to obesity. Certain bacteria have a tendency to harvest more energy from the foods we consume, and the more energy we absorb, the more likely we are to become overweight.

Now things get really crazy: Studies have shown that by taking the gut bacteria of a fat mouse and putting it into a skinny mouse—use your imagination—the skinny mouse gets fatter within weeks.[18] In another study, researchers spiked the drinks of obese mice with a healthy strain of bacteria harvested from skinny mice and the fat mice lost weight.[19] The researchers discovered that the new healthy bacteria created chemicals in the gut of the fat mice that told their Limbo that they weren't so hungry anymore and they ate less food—recall from Chapter 4 that the Limbo is involved in the drive to eat. What this and many other studies are showing is that our gut can have a profound effect on our Limbo, so much so that the gut has been referred to as the "second brain."[20] It has even been argued that this is why we sometimes get "gut feelings" about certain decisions.[21]

Scientists have discovered that our gut can affect our brain through two mechanisms.[22] First, there are nerves that lead from our gut to our Limbo.[23] Studies have identified that bugs in the gut can migrate up these nerves—such as the vagus nerve—and wreak havoc with our Limbo.[24] Second, the state of our gut can affect our state of mind through chemicals produced by our gut bacteria that are absorbed into our blood and make their way to the Limbo. Because of this gut–brain connection, a poor diet can actually shrink parts of our Limbo![25]

What all this means is that we want those little critters "down there" to be happy and healthy so we can be too. Some of our best friends can be germs! The best way to ensure their happiness is to feed them well. And there is a simple way to do that.

Make fibre your friend

The gut bacteria we have been learning about live a long way from our mouth, where food deliveries are made into our body. They mostly live in our large intestine, the last part of our 9 metres of gastrointestinal tract. Because they are last in line, it is easy for them to miss out on their share of the good stuff, if there is not enough of it in our diet. And if you have ever tried living in a house with a few hungry kids, you know that it is not a happy place. Living with trillions of them can be a disaster!

Fortunately, nature provided an easy way for us to keep them happy, so we can be happy too. The magic ingredient is fibre! Fibre is the non-digestible parts of plants—there is no

Fibre is the non-digestible parts of plants—there is no fibre in animal products—and our gut bacteria love the stuff.

fibre in animal products—and our gut bacteria love the stuff! As it is non-digestible, it passes through the length of our gastrointestinal tract and arrives intact at our colon, where the bacteria feed on it.

Unfortunately, most people today starve their gut bacteria. The Standard American Diet—endemic in most western and now many developing countries—is highly processed. Processing strips the fibre out of it. This has resulted in an incredible but little-known statistic: 97 per cent of people don't consume the recommended daily intake of fibre.[26] This makes for a lot of unhappy gut bacteria! The absurdity is that we are constantly told to eat more protein, despite the fact that 97 per cent of people *do* get enough of it, including vegetarians.[27] By contrast, while the vast majority of people don't consume anywhere near

the recommended amounts of fibre, we hear little about it.

There is some evidence that taking probiotics, which help put good bacteria into our gut, can actually decrease symptoms of anxiety, depression, anger and hostility.[28] But the consensus among the experts is that feeding the good bacteria we already have so that it can flourish is a better way to go.[29]

The takeaway message is that we need to make fibre our friend if we want to give our Limbo a lift, and the best way to do that is to consume more whole plant foods in as close to their natural state as possible. They should look like they came from a farm, not a factory!

There are two other things we need to know about making the most of fibre. First, different plant foods contain different types of fibre—and other nutrients—and their colour leaves clues. So, by eating plant foods of a variety of colours, we eat more nutritiously, which pleases our gut bacteria. Think of it this way: Just as our taste buds would get bored with being served up the same-old-same-old, so do our gut bacteria! We should try to *eat a rainbow* by consuming whole plant-based foods of a variety of colours. Our gut bacteria will be happier and our Limbo will be too!

Finally, when we consume a high-fibre diet, we need to drink plenty of water. Many plant foods take care of that by having a naturally high water content, but it is a good idea to make a concerted effort to drink eight to 10 glasses of water a day anyway. In its own right, drinking more water can go a long way toward making us feel better because our brain—including our Limbo—is very sensitive to dehydration.[30] In fact, our brain is about 75 per cent water and studies have shown that it actually shrinks—literally shrivels—when we are dehydrated.[31] Understandably, this can have a big effect on how we feel.

The point is to make sure you drink eight to 10 glasses of water each day so you are well hydrated. As a tip, you know you are sufficiently well hydrated if your urine is clear, so *don't go for the gold!*

There is now overwhelming evidence to highlight the fact that *food feeds our mood*—and to understand why, we had to venture to the furthest regions of our gut!

It's undeniable: To *live more*, we need to *eat more* plants.

Putting it into action

1. Eight fists full of fibre.

Each day, try to consume eight—or more—serves of whole, plant-based foods that come in four varieties: fruits, vegetables, whole grains and legumes (beans).

Here are a few tips:

- A "serve" is the size of your fist (or bigger).
- They should be consumed in as close to their natural state as possible.
- Breads count as long as they are wholegrain or wholemeal.

2. Masterchef me.

Take a step toward being a Masterchef by cooking and sharing a plant-based meal. There are plenty of plant-based cookbooks available, so you should have no trouble getting your hands on one. Two of my favourites are *Simple, Tasty, Good* and *Food As Medicine*. Hopefully, you will enjoy these so much that cooking good food will become a regular part of your eating plan. Your gut bacteria and Limbo will love you for it and, by sharing the meal, you will be giving someone else's Limbo a lift too!

Recap

There is an intimate connection between our Limbo and gut because of the influence the trillions of bacteria that live "down there" have on our brain. To keep our gut bacteria happy, so that we can be happy, we need to *eat nutritiously*. By eating more plant foods, which are high in fibre, we feed our friendly gut bacteria that in turn help us live more!

1. S Anders, M Tanaka and D K Kinney (2013), "Depression as an evolutionary strategy for defense against infection," *Brain, Behavior, and Immunity*, 31, pages 9–22.

2. ibid.

3. M Pollan (2008), *In Defense of Food*, Penguin Press.

4. D Morton, P Rankin, L Kent and W Dysinger (2014), "The Complete Health Improvement Program (CHIP): History, Evaluation, and Outcomes," *American Journal of Lifestyle Medicine*, 10(1), pages 64–73.

5. C L Thieszen, R M Merrill, S G Aldana, D A Vermeersch, R M Merrill, H A Diehl, R L Greenlaw and H Englert (2011), "The Coronary Health Improvement Project (CHIP) for lowering weight and improving psychosocial health," *Psychological Reports*, 109, pages 338–52.

6. B L Beezhold, C S Johnston and D R Daigle (2010), "Vegetarian diets are associated with healthy mood states: A cross-sectional study in Seventh Day Adventist adults," *Nutrition Journal*, 9, page 26; J S Lai, S Hiles, A Bisquera, A J Hure, M McEvoy and J Attia (2014), "A systematic review and meta-analysis of dietary patterns and depression in community-dwelling adults," *American Journal of Clinical Nutrition*, 99(1), pages 181–97; S E McMartin, F N Jacka and I Colman (2013), "The association between fruit and vegetable consumption and mental health disorders: Evidence from five waves of a national survey of Canadians," *Preventive Medicine*, 56, pages 225–30; M E Payne, S E Steck, R R George and D C Steffens (2012), "Fruit, Vegetable and Antioxidant Intakes are Lower in Older Adults with Depression," *Journal of the Academy of Nutrition and Dietetics*, 112(12), pages 2022–7.

7. D G Blanchflower, A J Oswald and S Stewart-Brown (2013), "Is Psychological Well-Being Linked to the Consumption of Fruit and Vegetables?" *Social Indicators Research*, 114, pages 785–801.

8. B A White, C C Horwath and T S Conner (2013), "Many apples a day keep the blues away: Daily experiences of negative and positive affect and food consumption in young adults," *British Journal of Health Psychology*, 18, pages 782–98.

9. F Jacka, A O'Neil, R Opi, C Itsiopoulos, S Cotton, M Mohebbi, D Castle, S Dash, C Mihalopoulos, M L Chatterton, L Brazionis, O M Dean, A M Hodge and M Berk (2017), "A randomised controlled trial of dietary improvement for adults with major depression (the 'SMILES' trial)," *BMC Medicine*, 15, page 23.

10. T S Conner, K L Brookie, A C Richardson and M A Polak (2015), "On carrots and curiosity: Eating fruit and vegetables is associated with greater flourishing in daily life," *British Journal of Health Psychology*, 20(2), pages 413–27; R Mujcic (2014), "Are fruit and vegetables good for our mental and physical health? Panel data evidence from Australia," MPRA Paper No. 59149.

11. B L Beezhold and C S Johnston (2012), "Restriction of meat, fish, and poultry in omnivores improves mood: A pilot randomized controlled trial," *Nutrition Journal*, 11, page 9.

12. M H Bloch and J Hannestad (2012), "Omega-3 fatty acids for the treatment of depression: Systematic review and meta-analysis," *Molecular Psychiatry*, 17, pages 1272–82.

13. T C Campbell and H Jacobson (2013), *Whole: Rethinking the Science of Nutrition*, BenBella Books.

14. P Holford (2003), "Depression: The nutrition connection," *Primary Care Mental Health*, 1, pages 9–16.

15. E M M Quigley (2013), "Gut Bacteria in Health and Disease," *Gastroenterology & Hepatology*, 9(9), pages 560–9.

16. E A Mayer (2011), "Gut feelings: The emerging biology of gut-brain communication," *Nature Reviews: Neuroscience*, 12, pages 453–66.

17. J C Clemente, L K Ursell, L W Parfrey and R Knight (2012), "The Impact of the Gut Microbiota on Human Health: An Integrative View," *Cell*, 148, pages 1258–70.

18. P J Turnbaugh, R E Ley, M A Mahowald, V Magrini, E R Mardis and J I Gordon (2006), "An obesity-associated gut microbiome with increased capacity for energy harvest," *Nature*, 444(7122), pages 1027–31.

19. Z Chen, L Guo, Y Zhang, R L Walzem, J S Pendergast, R L Printz, L C Morris, E Matafonova, X Stien, L Kang, D Coulon, O P McGuinness, K D Niswender and S S Davies (2014), "Incorporation of therapeutically modified bacteria into gut microbiota inhibits obesity," *Journal of Clinical Investigation*, 124(8), pages 3391–3406.

20. A Hadhazy (2010), "Think Twice: How the Gut's 'Second Brain' Influences Mood and Well-Being," *Scientific American*, February 12, <www.scientificamerican.com/article/gut-second-brain/>.

21. E Mayer (2011), "Gut feelings: The emerging biology of gut-brain communication," *Nature Reviews Neuroscience*, 12, pages 453–66.

22. J Cryan (2015), "Food for thought: How gut microbes can change your mind," TEDMED, <http://tedmed.com/talks/show?id=293045>.

23. F Gomez-Pinilla (2008), "Brain foods: The effects of nutrients on brain function," *Nature Reviews: Neuroscience*, 9, pages 568–78.

24. J A Bravo, P Forsythe, M V Chewb, E Escaravage, H M Savignaca, T G Dinana, J Bienenstock and J F Cryana (2011), "Ingestion of Lactobacillus strain regulates emotional behavior and central GABA receptor expression in a mouse via the vagus nerve," *Proceedings of the National Academy of Sciences*, 108(38), pages 16050–5.

25. F N Jacka, N Cherbuin, K J Anstey, P Sachdev and P Butterworth (2015), "Western diet is associated with a smaller hippocampus: A longitudinal investigation," *BMC Medicine*, 13, page 215.

26. R Clemens, S Kranz, A R Mobley, T A Nicklas, M P Raimondi, J C Rodriguez, J L Slavin and H Warshaw (2012), "Filling America's Fiber

Intake Gap: Summary of a Roundtable to Probe Realistic Solutions with a Focus on Grain-Based Foods," *Journal of Nutrition*, 142(7), pages 1390S-401S.

27. NHANES (2005), "What we eat in America," <www.ars.usda.gov/SP2UserFiles/Place/80400530/pdf/0102/usualintaketables2001-02.pdf>.

28. M Messaoudi (2011), "Assessment of psychotropic-like properties of a probiotic formulation (Lactobacillus helveticus R0052 and Bifidobacterium longum R0175) in rats and human subjects," *British Journal of Nutrition*, 105, pages 755–64.

29. M Pollan (2013), "Some of my best friends are germs," *New York Times,* <www.nytimes.com/2013/05/19/magazine/say-hello-to-the-100-trillion-bacteria-that-make-up-your-microbiome.html>.

30. N A Masento, M Golightly, D T Field, L T Butler and C M van Reekum (2014), "Effects of hydration status on cognitive performance and mood," *British Journal of Nutrition*, 111(10), pages 1841–52.

31. ibid.

S·M·I·L·**E**·R·S

EAT NUTRITIOUSLY

Chapter 8

Rest to feel our best

—Rest: Sleep—

The very best way to lengthen the day is to steal a few hours from the night.—Sir Henry Norman

Sometimes I wake up cranky; sometimes I just let him sleep.—Anonymous

Have you ever been so tired that you could hardly keep your eyes open? Isn't it a terrible feeling? I especially hate it when it happens in meetings. I am meant to be interested and attentive, but my eyes are so heavy that I would give anything to close them. But I know that if I let my eyelids meet, I might not have the strength to part them again and, a moment later, I would be slumped over on the desk with everyone watching with disdain.

Studies indicate that one of the best ways to become sleep deprived is to have children. It is estimated that parents of a new baby forego between 400 and 750 hours of sleep in the first year alone.[1] From my experience, this seems a conservative estimate!

I remember when my eldest—Olivia—was about six months old, and she had my wife and me up most of the night for more than a week. I felt absolutely haggard. One night toward the end of that week, I was standing beside her crib at 3 am as she incessantly screamed and thought to myself, *I am going to die from sleep deprivation*. It felt like my body was shutting down. My brain certainly had.

The only thing that kept me upright at that moment was the escalating screaming, which eventually caused me to look down and notice that I was holding the dummy in her eye socket rather than her mouth. Fortunately, today she is a happy and healthy teenager with 20/20 vision—and she hardly ever wakes us during the night!

In this chapter, we will look at the growing problem that is sleep deprivation, how it affects our Limbo—why we feel so lousy when we go without sleep—and what we can do about it.

Just lie down and go to sleep!

Sleep is a fascinating and bizarre behaviour. We race around all day with our schedule planned to the last minute as if we don't have a moment to spare, then we lie down and hibernate for several hours. The average person sleeps 36 per cent of their life, which means that if we make it to 90 years old, we will have spent 32 of those years asleep.[2] Not surprisingly, some individuals, such as Thomas Jefferson, have viewed sleep as a pointless waste of time and attempted to function on very little. But sleep has a powerful allure and such individuals become known for napping in order to keep functioning.

Despite our obsession with sleep—after all, we can't stop doing it!—scientists don't have a good understanding of why we sleep. What we do know is that we definitely need it and things go badly for us if we go for too long without it—in fact, it can kill us. This is tragically played out in an incredibly rare condition suffered by members of a certain Spanish family. The condition is called "fatal familial insomnia" and, in unfortunate family members, a "sleepless switch" turns on inside them and they simply can't sleep at all.[3] Death follows within months and, while the exact cause of death is uncertain, autopsies show extensive damage to the Limbo, which hints at the influence of sleeplessness on this part of our brain.

Despite the known perils of going without sleep, some people have still tested the limits. One of the most notable cases is that of Randy Gardner who, in 1964, decided to go without sleep for 11 days—264 hours—for a science experiment. Pioneering sleep researcher Dr William Dement heard about the attempt and enthusiastically volunteered to "support" Randy, along with a couple of Randy's friends, to stay true to the course. Randy's support crew "helped" him stay awake by making him play basketball at 3 am, walking him around the block and, when all else failed, by standing directly in front of him and screaming "Open your eyes, open your eyes, you can do it!" Randy would slur back, "Why are you doing this to me?" After four days, Randy even became delusional, thinking he was someone he wasn't and mistaking road signs for people.

Randy described the experiment as fun and exciting at first but, as the sleep deprivation kicked in—to use his words—it became "a real bummer." And that is how our Limbo feels about sleep deprivation.

Note: Due to the perils of sleep deprivation, the *Guinness Book of World Records* no longer accepts claims for the longest duration without sleep.

There is no doubt that lack of sleep affects our entire body, including our brain. We don't have to go long without enough sleep before problems begin to appear. After only 17 to 19 hours without sleep, our ability to react and respond can be compromised by 50 per cent and our performance can be worse than having a blood alcohol limit above the legal driving limit of 0.05 per cent.[4] So it is hardly surprising that many accounts of major accidents, such as oil tankers running aground and planes crashing, have been linked to lack of sleep. Even the devastating Challenger Space Shuttle accident has been traced back to crucial errors of judgment attributed to sleep deprivation.[5]

It is important to note that it is not only complete sleep deprivation that causes issues. "Sleep restriction"—when we don't get enough sleep for several nights in a row—can be equally damaging. Researchers from the University of Pennsylvania

After only a few days of being sleep restricted, the participants seemed to lose their ability to judge how sleepy or poorly performing they actually were.

and Harvard Medical School teamed up to compare the effects of total sleep deprivation to prolonged sleep restriction. In the study, the subjects slept for only four or six hours each night for 14 days.[6] Not surprisingly, those who only had four hours of sleep each night suffered greater cognitive deficits than those who had six hours of sleep each night. But after two weeks, even those who were restricted to six hours sleep per night had reductions in their cognitive ability equivalent to not sleeping at all for two days. Even more interesting, after only a few days of being sleep restricted, the participants seemed to lose their ability to judge how sleepy or poorly performing they actually were—it seemed they had lost their reference from what it felt like to be fully awake and functional!

In addition to the greater risk of accidents, lack of sleep causes real changes in the workings of our body. Sleep deprivation is related to type 2 diabetes, cardiovascular disease and premature death from all causes.[7]

If this isn't bad enough, lack of sleep wreaks havoc on our Limbo as a result of a number of chemicals produced by various parts of the body and brain when we are tired. One of these chemicals is ghrelin, known as the "hunger hormone." Our stomach normally produces ghrelin when it is empty and sends this chemical messenger to the Limbo, which in turn motivates us to eat. As our happy stomach fills up, it stops producing ghrelin and our Limbo tones down the feeding impulse.

But when we are sleep deprived, our stomach ramps up its production of ghrelin, even when it is not empty.[8] Hence, sleep deprivation results in overeating—and we know what that means. Yes, lack of sleep can make us fat![9]

Of course, too much sleeping and lying around can do likewise. This is why the Wisconsin Sleep Cohort Study found a U-shaped relationship between how much people sleep on average and their body mass index, which is a measure of overweight and obesity. Individuals who got 7.7 hours of sleep on a typical night had the lowest body mass indexes. Body weight went up for both the shorter and longer sleepers, but the increase in weight was most pronounced for the shorter sleepers.[10] The influence of sleep deprivation on obesity is so well established that the worldwide obesity epidemic we are witnessing has been attributed to a reduction in our average sleep time over the past few decades.[11]

How being sleep-deprived affects our Limbo

Our Limbo takes a hit when we are tired. Recall from Chapter 1 that our Limbo has several functions, represented by "Hmmm": It is our **H**ome of happy (meaning our emotions), **m**emory, **m**otivation and in charge of **m**any automatic bodily processes, including our immune system. All these functions are impaired by lack of sleep.[12]

With regard to *memory*, countless studies have shown that sleep facilitates the formation of memories and so improves learning.[13] In a study at the University of Alberta, researchers gave study participants some things to remember, then instructed half of them to go have a nap before returning 12 hours later for a memory quiz. The other participants were told to avoid napping but that they would receive a financial reward for every answer they got right in the quiz.[14] The researchers found that, when it came to boosting memory, the nap worked better than the cash prize! This is not so surprising as it is known that new neurons are generated in the Limbo during sleep and lack of sleep slows down that process.[15]

> *New neurons are generated in the Limbo during sleep and lack of sleep slows down that process.*

With regard to *motivation*, I don't need to cite studies as evidence that motivation levels plummet when we are sleepy. We can all attest to this from personal experience!

Finally, there are now numerous studies demonstrating that sleep deprivation affects *many automatic bodily processes*, especially our immune system, which means that sleeplessness can result in sickness.[16]

So memory, motivation and many automatic bodily processes—

all functions of our Limbo—are affected by our sleep status. But most relevant to our interest in being emotionally up and living more is the effect of sleep deprivation on the Limbo's main function, which is mood. I am sure I don't need to convince you of the fact that, when we are tired, we feel lousy. Think back to the last time you were really tired and reflect on whether or not you felt full of the joy of living.

Certainly, sleep deprivation is linked to low mood and depression[17]—but what comes first? While the two probably affect each other, several studies show that when we are sleep deprived our brains are geared toward the negative. In one study, the researchers compared the activity of the part of the Limbo involved in processing negative emotions in people who had a good night sleep with those who were sleep deprived. Using MRI scans, they found, that this part of the Limbo "lit up" more in the group that were sleep deprived when they were shown aversive images.[18]

In another study, people were shown and asked to remember a group of random words after a good sleep and then when they were sleep deprived. The participants were not alerted to the fact that some of the words they were shown were positive—"smile", "happy", "calm"—others negative—"grief", "angry", "crash"—and the remaining neutral—"door", "carpet", "wheel". The researchers found that participants were more than twice as likely to remember the negative words in the sleepy state.[19]

What these studies show is that our Limbo is highly influenced by our state of sleep, so in order to live more, we need to make sure we rest well.

So are you getting enough? And if not, what can you do about it?

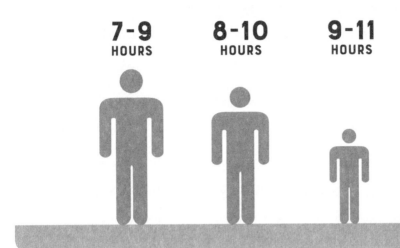

I'm so tired but I just can't fall asleep!

How many hours of sleep do you get on an average night? The consensus of the Expert Panel of the National Sleep Foundation recommends nine to 11 hours each night for school-aged children, eight to 10 hours for teenagers, and seven to nine hours for adults.[20]

Despite these sleep needs, surveys conducted in the United States suggest that nearly 30 per cent of adults sleep six hours or less each night[21] and less than one-third of high school students reported getting at least eight hours of sleep on an average school night.[22] Chances are you are sleep deprived.

Ironically, while so many people are in need of sleep, they struggle to nod off when the opportunity presents. Studies indicate that about one in 20 adults in the United States have popped a pill in the past month to help them sleep.[23]

A number of factors seem to be contributing to our sleepless society, but let's consider three of the most notable:

Sleep-stealing Culprit 1: Physical inactivity

The downturn in our physical activity levels, as we learned about in Chapter 3, might be contributing to poorer sleep habits. You have probably experienced it for yourself that when we have an active day we sleep better that night. This anecdotal experience is backed up by studies that show increasing our physical activity levels is an excellent way to improve sleep quality.[24] However, as exercise makes people feel more alert, some people find it difficult to fall asleep if they exercise too close to bed time, so it is recommended that exercise be performed earlier in the day.

Sleep-stealing Culprit 2: Caffeine

The increasingly widespread use of caffeine—doubling in the past 30 years—might be contributing to insomnia. Around 85 per cent of people use caffeinated products every day in the United States[25] and the rates of usage are probably similar in most developed countries, making it the most commonly used psychoactive drug in the world. So how does caffeine work?

Over the course of the day, there is the progressive accumulation of a chemical in our brain called adenosine. When the levels get high, we feel sleepy. When we go to sleep, the adenosine levels come down and we wake up feeling refreshed. But caffeine blocks the receptors in our brain that detect adenosine. Therefore, even though the adenosine levels might be high, our brain doesn't register it, so we don't feel tired.[26]

But this scenario is like putting our hand over the "low fuel" light when it comes on in our car and thinking the problem is solved as we continue to charge on down the freeway. Because we keep charging on, the adenosine levels continue to accumulate and we are going to have to stop to sleep at some point. But caffeine makes it harder to fall asleep and then reduces our ability to enter the deeper and more restorative levels of sleep that clears the adenosine.[27]

When the adenosine is not properly cleared, we wake up feeling lousy and need more caffeine to block the receptors and get going again! In the long-term, caffeine use doesn't actually give us higher highs, it just brings us back up to a normal level—that which would be our normal if we weren't regularly using caffeine. People dependent on caffeine only think it causes a "high" because without it they are flat.

Caffeine is an insomnia culprit, even for morning-only users, since its stimulating effects can persist for up to 14 hours.[28]

Sleep-stealing Culprit 3: Night light pollution

Arguably the single biggest contributor to the demise of our sleep was the invention of the light bulb—thanks for nothing, Thomas Edison! The light bulb gave us the ability to make night seem like day and we have seized the opportunity to extend our days. It has allowed us to go to bed later, and since we still have to get up at much the same time, we sleep less. Today, more than 99 per cent of people living in developed countries are exposed to what is labelled "night light pollution." Intriguingly, the increasing rate of depression over the past few decades parallels the increased exposure of many to light at night.[29]

So why is night light referred to as *pollution*? Our Limbo has an in-built clock called the *suprachiasmatic nucleus*, but we can call it the SCN for short. The SCN is in charge of setting our sleep-wake cycles, also known as our *biorhythms* or *circadian* rhythms.[30] These rhythms follow a 24-hour cycle (almost) and dictate when we feel sparky and when we feel sedate. This is why it is possible to have a lot of sleep one night and still feel

tired, or to have little sleep and still feel quite perky—the highs and lows of our biorhythms have a major impact on how tired we feel.

To help us cope better with the changing seasons, the SCN has the ability to tweak our sleep-wake cycle. This is a good thing because otherwise we couldn't get over *jet lag* when we travel to distant lands, which results when we travel quickly to a different time zone and our biorhythms are out of sync with the destination. To keep tabs on when it should make us feel awake, the SCN notices the amount of light that comes in contact with our eyes, especially "blue light" which appears in the morning.[31] Essentially, the SCN is clever enough to know that bright blue light means morning time, so it starts a wake cycle, causing us to rise and shine.

The problem today is that we have access to bright light in the evening at the flick of a switch, which can confuse the SCN into thinking it is time to wake. To make matters worse, screens emit blue light, so the SCN is tricked doubly when we use computers, smart phones and tablets at night. To help counter this, we can buy glasses that block blue light and some devices now have a function that shifts the light they emit away from the blue end of the spectrum.

Before the electric light bulb, we relied on fire for our light. Firelight is relatively dim and has no tinge of blue to it—it is a red light. This type of light results in the production of a chemical called melatonin, produced by the pineal gland in our brain, which causes the SCN to slow down and make us weary.

A study conducted by researchers at the University of Colorado highlighted how the modern electrical lighting environment conspires against us and how therapeutic natural light can be.[32] The researchers took people camping for a week, during which they were exposed to only natural light—sun, moon, stars and fire light—which resulted in no "blue" light exposure at night. Within days, the biorhythms of the participants

> *Artificial light at night wreaks havoc on our biorhythms.*

adjusted and they started going to sleep approximately two-and-a-half hours earlier than when they were exposed to artificial light before their camping trip.

In summary, artificial light at night wreaks havoc on our biorhythms. Our poor little SCN doesn't know whether to make us sleepy or sprightly. Is it any wonder that so many people are struggling to sleep? So what can we do about it?

Tips for sleeping better

Considered a father of sleep research, Dr William Dement writes in the opening page of his book *The Promise of Sleep*, "After all the research I've done on sleep problems over the past four decades, my most significant finding is that ignorance is the worst sleep disorder of them all. People lack the most basic information about how to manage their sleep, leading to a huge amount of unnecessary suffering."[33] So what are the lessons we can take away to improve the quality of our sleep?

Here are some tips from the National Institutes of Health:[34]

1. **Get the light right.** Avoid bright—especially blue—light at night.

2. **Be active in the morning light.** We have learned that both morning light and exercise are great for improving sleep. Why not combine the two, if you can, for a double bonus?

3. **Stick to a sleep schedule.** Go to bed and wake up at much the same time each day, if you can—even on weekends. Keeping a regular sleep-wake cycle helps our bio-clock—the SCN—to get a good routine of knowing when to make us feel sleepy and when to make us feel awake.

4. **Avoid things that keep you up.** There are a lot of things that can keep us up at night and make it hard to fall asleep. As we have already seen, caffeine is clearly one of them. Exercising and eating too late in the evening can also have stimulating effects on some people. Contrary to popular thought, alcoholic drinks are not helpful for getting good sleep. While a "nightcap" might help you fall asleep, the alcohol keeps you in the lighter stages of sleep, so the sleep you get is not as good quality.[35]

   Day-time naps have been shown to be highly beneficial, even if only 10 minutes in duration.[36] But longer than

30 minutes can interfere with our sleep-wake cycle and make it more difficult to fall asleep, especially if they occur later in the afternoon or evening.

Finally, many people today suffer from a condition referred to as FoMO—Fear of Missing Out—which we mentioned in Chapter 5.[37] They find it difficult to drag themselves away from the internet, social media and television for fear of what they might miss. If that is you, I promise that it will still be there in the morning—so go to bed!

5. **Make your sleep environment the most relaxing place on the planet.** Everything about our sleeping space should be relaxing—after all, we spend about one-third of our life there! Make sure your bed is comfortable and do what you can to make it a dark and quiet place. And before you get into bed, take time to relax, whether it be reading a book—not on a screen—listening to music or having a bath.

Sleep is so important for our health and wellbeing that we can't afford not to make it a priority. If you struggle to get enough quality sleep, take measures to remedy it. Try the strategies above and, if they are not helpful, talk with your healthcare provider.

Putting it into action

1. TIB-8.

TIB stands for "Time in Bed"[38] and the "8" refers to eight hours. This week, endeavour to spend eight hours in bed each night. You don't have to be sleeping—you can read or whatever, as long as it does not involve a screen—but endeavour to be in bed for a full eight hours. (Of course, you can get up for bathroom visits.) Take notice of how prioritising TIB makes you feel.

2. Night by firelight.

Switch off all electric lights for a night (except in the case of emergency). Ideally, find somewhere safe and legal that you can have a campfire and sit around it with friends. If you can't enjoy a campfire, then light candles in your home. Take note of how the mood changes by firelight.

> **Recap**
>
> Many people today are sleep deprived, and this is bad news for their Limbo and hence how they feel. Many aspects of modern living set us up for poor sleep, artificial light being a significant contributor. To help us feel better and live more, we need to prioritise sleep and get the light right!

1. National Sleep Research Project, <www.abc.net.au/science/sleep/facts.htm>.

2. R Foster (2013), "Why do we sleep?" TEDGlobal, <www.ted.com/talks/russell_foster_why_do_we_sleep?>.

3. C Tabernero, J M Polo, M D Sevillano, R Munoz, J Berciano, A Cabello, B Baez, J R Ricoy, R Carpizo, J Figols, N Cuadrado and L E Claveria (2000), "Fatal familial insomnia: clinical, neuropathological, and genetic description of a Spanish family," *Journal of Neurology, Neurosurgery & Psychiatry*, 68, pages 774–7.

4. A M Williamson and A M Feyer (2000), "Moderate sleep deprivation produces impairments in cognitive and motor performance equivalent to legally prescribed levels of alcohol intoxication," *Occupational and*

Environmental Medicine, 57, pages 649–55.

5. National Sleep Foundation, <www.sleepfoundation.org/>.

6. H P A Van Dongen, G Maislin, J M Mullington and D F Dinges (2003), "The cumulative cost of additional wakefulness: Dose-response effects on neurobehavioral functions and sleep physiology from chronic sleep restriction and total sleep deprivation," *Sleep*, 2, pages 117–26.

7. K L Chien, P C Chen, H C Hsu, T C Su, F C Sung, M F Chen and Y T Lee (2010), "Habitual sleep duration and insomnia and the risk of cardio-vascular events and all-cause death: Report from a community-based cohort," *Sleep*, 33, pages 177–84; L Gallicchio and B Kalesan (2009), "Sleep duration and mortality: A systematic review and meta-analysis," *Journal of Sleep Research*, 18, pages 148–58.

8. C Benedict, S J Brooks, O G O'Daly, M S Almèn, A Morell, K Åberg, M Gingnell, B Schultes, M Hallschmid, J E Broman, E M Larsson and H B Schiöth (2012), "Acute Sleep Deprivation Enhances the Brain's Response to Hedonic Food Stimuli: An fMRI Study," *The Journal of Clinical Endocrinology & Metabolism*, 97(3), pages E443–7.

9. L L Morselli, A Guyon and K Spiegel (2012), "Sleep and metabolic function," *European Journal of Physiology*, 463, pages 139–60.

10. S Taheri, L Lin, D Austin, T Young and E Mignot (2004), "Short sleep duration is associated with reduced leptin, elevated ghrelin, and increased body mass index," *PLoS Medicine*, 1(3), page e62.

11. E Van Cauter and K L Knutson (2008), "Sleep and the epidemic of obesity in children and adults," *European Journal of Endocrinology*, 159, pages S59–S66.

12. R Stickgold (2015), "Sleep on it!" *New Scientist*, 313(4), pages 52–7.

13. Foster, op cit.

14. M A Tucker, S X Tang, A Uzoh, A Morgan and R Stickgold (2011), "To Sleep, to Strive, or Both: How Best to Optimize Memory," *PLoS ONE*, 6(7), e21737.

15. P Meerlo, R E Mistlberger, B L Jacobs, H C Heller and D McGinty (2009), "New neurons in the adult brain: The role of sleep and consequences of sleep loss," *Sleep Medicine Reviews*, 13, pages 187–94.

16. P A Bryant, J Trinder and N Curtis (2004), "Sick and tired: Does sleep have a vital role in the immune system?" *Nature Reviews*, 4, pages 457–67.

17. D Neckelmann, A Mykletun and A A Dahl (2007), "Chronic Insomnia As a Risk Factor for Developing Anxiety and Depression," *Sleep*, 30(7), pages 873–80.

18. S Yoo, N Gujar, P Hu, F Jolesz and P Walker (2007), "The human emotional brain without sleep—a prefrontal amygdala disconnect," *Current Biology*, 17(20), pages R877–8.

19. Stickgold, op cit.

20. M Hirshkowitz, K Whiton, S M Albert, CAlessi, O Bruni, L DonCarlos, N Hazen, J Herman, E S Katz, L Kheirandish-Gozal, D N Neubauer, A E O'Donnell, M Ohayon, J Peever, R Rawding, R C Sachdeva, B Setters, M V Vitiello, J C Ware and P J Adams Hillard (2015), "National Sleep Foundation's sleep time duration recommendations: Methodology and results summary," *Sleep Health*, 1, pages 40–3.

21. C A Schoenborn and P F Adams (2010), "Health behaviors of adults: United States, 2005–2007," National Center for Health Statistics, Vital & Health Statistics, 10(245).

22. Center for Disease Control and Prevention (2009), "Youth Risk Behavior Surveillance—United States, 2009," *Morbidity and Mortality Weekly Report*, 59, SS-5.

23. Y Chong, C D Fryar and Q Gu (2013), "Prescription sleep aid use among adults: United States 2005–2010," Center for Disease Control and Prevention, <www.cdc.gov/nchs/data/databriefs/db127.pdf>.

24. M P Buman A C King (2010), "Exercise as a Treatment to Enhance Sleep," *American Journal of Lifestyle Medicine*, 4, pages 500–14.

25. D C Mitchell, C A Knight, J Hockenberry, R Teplansky and T J Hartman (2014), "Beverage caffeine intakes in the US," *Food and Chemical Toxicology*, 63, pages 136–42.

26. R Basheer, R E Strecker, M M Thakkar and R W McCarley (2004), "Adenosine and sleep–wake regulation," *Progress in Neurobiology*, 73, pages 379–96.

27. T Roehrs and T Roth (2008), "Caffeine: Sleep and daytime sleepiness," *Sleep Medicine Reviews*, 12, pages 153–62.

28. T M Heffron (2013), "Sleep and Caffeine," American Academy of Sleep Medicine, <www.sleepeducation.org/news/2013/08/01/sleep-and-caffeine>.

29. T A Bedrosian and R J Nelson (2013), "Influence of the modern light environment on mood," *Molecular Psychiatry*, 18, pages 751–7.

30. P C Zee and P Manthena (2007), "The brain's master circadian clock: Implications and opportunities for therapy of sleep disorders," *Sleep Medicine Reviews*, 11, pages 59–70.

31. Bedrosian and Nelson, op cit.

32. E R Stothard, A W McHill, C M Depner, B R Birks, T M Moehlman, H K Ritchie, J R Guzzetti, E D Chinoy, M K LeBourgeois, J Axelsson and K P Wright Jr (2017), "Circadian Entrainment to the Natural Light-Dark Cycle across Seasons and the Weekend," *Current Biology*, 27, pages 1–6.

33. W C Dement and C Vaughan (1999), *The Promise of Sleep: A Pioneer in Sleep Medicine Explores the Vital Connection Between Health, Happiness, and*

a Good Night's Sleep, Dell Trade Paperbacks, page 2.

34. National Institutes of Health (2012), "Your guide to healthy sleep," <www.nhlbi.nih.gov/sleep>.

35. I O Ebrahim, C M Shapiro, A J Williams and P B Fenwick (2013), "Alcohol and Sleep I: Effects on Normal Sleep," *Alcoholism: Clinical and Experimental Research*, 37(4), pages 539–49.

36. A Brooks and L Lack (2006), "A brief afternoon nap following nocturnal sleep restriction: Which nap duration is most recuperative?" *Sleep*, 29(6), pages 831–40.

37. Australian Psychological Association (2015), "Stress and Wellbeing: How Australians are coping with life," <www.psychology.org.au/psychologyweek/survey/>.

38. S Banks and D F Dinges (2007), "Behavioral and physiological consequences of sleep restriction," *Journal of Clinical Sleep Medicine,* 3(5), pages 519–28.

S·M·I·L·E·R·S

 **REST WELL: SLEEP**

Chapter 9

Stress less

–Rest: De-stress–

For the vast majority of beasts on this planet, stress is about a short-term crisis, after which it is over with or you're over with.— Robert Sapolsky

The only way to avoid being miserable is to not have enough leisure time to wonder whether you are happy or not. —George Bernard Shaw

Many years ago, when my brother and I were in our late teens, we were offered a two-for-one deal to go bungee jumping. How could we turn down an offer like that? On the way to the venue, our spirits were high and we bantered about who would go first, eventually agreeing that he would have the honour.

Arriving at the venue and looking up at the jump, he exclaimed, "You can go first!"

Soon I was sitting on a platform with a "bungee operator," attached to a crane that elevated us into the stratosphere—or so it seemed. As we ascended, the bungee operator strapped an oversized elastic band to my ankles and kept reiterating that the trick was to not look down.

Eventually, we came to a stop.

"I want you to stand up and look up at the camera positioned out front of the jumping ledge," he said. "Then slowly shuffle in that direction until I tell you to stop. And remember, just don't look down."

I followed all the instructions, except for the last one.

As soon as I peered down, I froze in terror. It was a long way to the ground below! My stomach lurched and I could literally hear my heart pounding in my chest. My palms began sweating profusely and my mouth went dry. With wide eyes, I turned to the operator and said, "I have made a big mistake. I can't do this!"

At this stage, the operator turned into a motivator and started to give me a rousing pep talk, which clearly he had done on many occasions before because he was very good at it! A few minutes later, he was giving me the big countdown, "Three, two, one . . . bungee!"

I would like to say that I performed a magnificent "swan dive" off the platform, but it was later described as more like a "chicken flap." As gravity took over, somewhat embarrassingly, I exhaled a pitiful squeal. It wasn't one of my finer moments, but fortunately my brother did no better.

In the moments before I "leapt"—if you could call it that—I was experiencing what is known as a "stress response." While the stress response isn't pleasant at the time—most of us don't enjoy feeling like we are about to throw up!—it is designed to help us in the face of threat and danger.

Throughout history, the way we dealt with stress-inducing circumstances was to fight or take flight, and the stress response helps us do this. Our heart rate is increased to help deliver oxygen to our soon-to-be fighting or fleeing body, and we start sweating to dissipate the heat we will soon be producing. In animals, the stress response can also cause them to "go to the bathroom" in order to lighten their load before the action begins. Humans usually manage to "hang on" but our gastrointestinal tract and bladder can still feel the pinch.

While the stress response is designed to help us in the moment, it is not helpful if it goes on too long. And this is where we come to a major problem. Many people today report high and ongoing levels of stress, more appropriately referred to as "distress."

An Australian study found that more than one in three adults report having a significant level of distress in their life.[1] Similarly, in the United States, four out of 10 employees say they typically feel tense or stressed during the workday, and stress costs more than $US300 billion a year as a result of absenteeism, turnover, diminished productivity, and medical, legal and insurance costs.[2] People report many sources of stress but the big ones relate to personal finances, family issues and health concerns.[3]

Intriguingly, the Australian Psychological Society found that one of the top five sources of stress, reported by 40 per cent of people, is "trying to maintain a healthy lifestyle."[4] In other words, we not only stress about things that are going wrong in our life, we also stress about things we might not be doing right.

Stress and worry seem to come too easy to us. A fascinating recent study has shown that, while stress affects our health, it is worse for people who believe that stress is damaging.[5] The takeaway message is that how we think about stress matters and stressing about being stressed makes things worse![6]

Calm down, Limbo, calm down!

Stress clearly involves the part of our brain responsible for feelings—we say, "I *feel* stressed!"—so we are talking again about our Limbo. So it is not surprising that stress—or more appropriately *distress*—affects all the other functions of the Limbo that we learned about in Chapter 1: Motivation, memory and many automatic bodily processes. In Chapter 1, we considered the effect of stress on automatic bodily processes involving our heart, gut and immune system, but let's briefly consider its affect on motivation and memory.

Stress has an interesting effect on our motivation—it normally causes us to go, go, go until we can't go anymore, after which we are unmotivated to do anything! This is analogous to the difference between anxiety and depression: Anxiety occurs when we are distressed but trying to do something about it; depression results when we are distressed but have given up trying.

A research student of mine conducted an interesting study that examined the influence of stress on our memory.[7] For the study, we recruited college students who were required to repetitively leap from a high platform—with ropes attached, of course—and we measured their stress levels, as well as their ability to remember things they had seen and heard immediately before leaping. We found that the more stressed they were, the less they could recall. You probably know this to be true from your own experience: As we become more panicked, our ability to process and remember information is compromised.

Throughout this book, we have been learning about the

> Stress has an interesting effect on our motivation—it normally causes us to go, go, go until we can't go anymore, after which we are unmotivated to do anything.

sources of input to our Limbo, both electrical and chemical, and how to use these sources to feel less down and more up. But these sources can also be used to combat unwanted feelings of distress. As we have seen, many people today need rest from stress, so let's look at how to achieve this using the SMILERS strategy—we will be considering the final "S" in the next chapter.

Turn down the heat! Open the valves!

When it comes to managing stress, there are two things we can do: We can turn down the heat by taking less on; or we can open the valves to relieve the pressure. Certainly, eliminating sources of stress from our life by saying "no" to certain things, lowering our expectations and not over-committing can go a long way toward decreasing stress in our life—it can turn down the heat. However, there are many things that we don't have control over and things often don't go to plan. People get sick, accidents happen, things break and deadlines are thrust upon us. So perhaps more important than removing stress from our lives is having the ability to relieve it. In other words, we can't always turn down the heat that causes the pressure, but we can adjust the valves.

Unfortunately, some of the strategies people resort to in an attempt to manage their stress also make the situation worse and can cause a lot of pain. An Australian report found that of those reporting severe stress, about 60 per cent drink alcohol, 40 per cent gamble, 40 per cent smoke, and 30 per cent take drugs to manage and cope.[8]

Thankfully, there are good and helpful ways to go about taking the pressure down.

SMILERS for de-stressing

In his classic book on stress, *Why Zebras Don't Get Stomach Ulcers*, stress researcher Robert Sapolsky makes the point that zebras do a lot right when it comes to managing stress.[9] Zebras have Limbos too, and they are very good at using the SMILERS approach to send it calming—or at least not distressing—messages. So let's learn from the zebra!

Speak positively

To the best of our knowledge, zebras don't wake up in the morning and immediately say to themselves, "I bet the lions are hungry today! It's been a couple of days since old Black Ears got taken. I have a bad feeling about it. I can see it now, those lions are going to come bounding down the hill when we are at the watering hole and I'll be last to see them coming. Plus, I stand out in the crowd for all the wrong reasons—I'm sure I am not as stripy as the others. Ahhh, this is bad, really bad! I'm a dead zebra walking!"

Zebras don't greet the day with that kind of negative talk. But do you? How often do you find yourself saying, both to yourself and others, "I've got to do this and I've got to do that, and this went wrong and that will probably go wrong, and there is not enough time in the day and . . ."?

Studies show that how we speak definitely influences our stress levels,[10] so be intentional about speaking positively. Practise the following: "I can get through this"; "It will be OK"; "Just one step at a time."

In this regard, we have an advantage over zebras. While they don't speak negatively, they also don't have the ability to speak positively. But you do, so why not do it?

Move dynamically

If you watch what happens after a zebra has just outrun a lion—lions give up pretty easily—you will notice something remarkable. The zebra will watch for a moment to make sure the lion has definitely called off the chase and is not just bluffing, then as the lion strolls back to its base with its tail between its legs, the zebra will put its head down and go back to its lunch. Can you believe it? It has just run for its life—literally—and shortly after doesn't appear stressed at all. How is this possible?

Recall that the stress response is designed to enable us for "fight or flight." All smart—and living—zebras choose the flight option when it comes to the lions. Essentially, the stress response gears us to do something physically active, as both fighting and fleeing are demanding physical pursuits. And here is the interesting thing: By doing something active, the stress response dials down. In effect, exercise "burns off" the stress. Exercise uses up what the stress response equips us to do. For the zebra, it is the act of running like their life depends on it that allows them to calm down and return to the important business of eating grass.

By contrast, modern humans tend to become more sedentary when they are stressed. A recent study indicated that the most popular way people endeavour to manage their stress is to *sit* and watch television or a movie.[11] In effect, they are doing the exact opposite of what the stress response is equipping them to do. Is it any wonder that stress levels remain so high?

We need to learn from the zebras. Instead of sitting in our stress, we need to *move dynamically*. Just one bout of exercise is enough to bring down our blood pressure.[12] I know that the busier I get, the more important it becomes for me to prioritise exercise. Doing something physically active is one of the best ways to open the valves when the pressure mounts.

Immerse in an uplifting physical and social environment

Zebras hang out in bright, sunny natural environments where there is plenty of blue and green. Their senses are bombarded with the uplifting sights, sounds and smells that natural landscapes provide. In short, blue and green is often seen by zebras!

Zebras are also social creatures that stay close and connected, without the use of social media! They have close-knit family units, which no doubt helps keep their stress levels down. They recognise that *together feels better*! We need to learn from zebras.

Look to the positive

While we can't be absolutely certain, Zebras don't seem to worry. They don't spiral down into negative thinking. It is believed that humans are the only species that worries, and it is arguably the greatest source of human suffering. The tragedy is that, while worry accounts for so much mental anguish, probably 90 per cent or more of what we worry about never actually happens. As Mark Twain once said, "I have known a great many troubles, but most of them never happened." Worry spends today's energy on tomorrow, which is unproductive, exhausting and stressful. A psychologist friend of mine says, "If and when it happens, you'll have plenty of time to worry about it then."

Zebras don't worry because they live in the moment, not the future. We humans can learn from this. It has been said that some people are so focused on the past that they walk backwards into the future. Living in the past can make us depressed. Others are so focused on the future that they fail to live in the present, and living in the future can make us anxious and stressed because the problem with living in the future is that there is just so much of it. When we look ahead, it is easy to become overwhelmed and alarmed—and the further we look, the worse our anticipation of it gets.

An increasingly popular activity used today to help pull us back into the "now" is the practice of mindfulness. Mindfulness is actually an ancient art that involves giving our attention to the present moment—being more "aware." In theory, it is simple, but it is challenging in practice, because our minds today are geared to be "mind full" rather than mindful. Importantly, mindfulness does not involve "emptying your mind" like some forms of meditation; rather, it involves giving more attention to what is happening "now" as compared to "then."

Being mindful can involve being more aware of what is going on around us or inside us. For example, in a natural environment, we might take notice of the sounds of birds or the feel of the wind. I consider photography a form of mindfulness as we concentrate our attention on a particular thing in space and time—a good thing—and our awareness increases and distractions disappear. It helps still our mind.

Being mindful of what is happening inside us might involve taking notice of whether our muscles are tense or relaxed, or whether our breathing is rapid and shallow or slow and full. Mindfulness activities have been shown to relieve stress and anxiety, and increase happiness.[13] Using a fMRI machine to observe the brain, researchers from the University of California found that practising mindfulness quite literally caused the Limbo to "calm down."[14] Zebras seem good at being mindful— they give their full attention to what is happening in the present—and we should learn from them.

But there is something else zebras seem to do that we could benefit from doing a lot more often than most of us do. Zebras are not only mindful of the moment; they also find it funny. Like all mammals, zebras laugh.[15] What tickles their funny bone is unclear, but it is likely good for them. To laugh is definitely good for us humans. Many studies show that humour and laughter boost our health, resilience and happiness. And it is a great way to relieve stress.[16] Wise Solomon was right when he wrote, "A merry heart doeth good like a medicine."[17]

All human groups laugh—there is not a culture or tribe that doesn't. Clearly we are meant to do it and we should—more often! How long has it been since you indulged in a good belly laugh? If you need help, studies indicate that we are about 30 times more likely to laugh when we are with others.[18] So seriously, find a funny friend and get a giggle going. Your stress levels will thank you for it.

> *Zebras are not only mindful of the moment; they also find it funny. Like all mammals, zebras laugh.*

Eat nutritiously

In case you haven't noticed, zebras eat nothing but high-fibre foods—it's called grass. I am not recommending we eat grass but, as we discovered in Chapter 7, there is evidence that eating a diet rich in plant foods helps with managing stress.[19] Unfortunately, these are often not the kind of foods people reach out for when they are stressed. When was the last time you heard someone say, "I am so stressed that I could eat an entire head of broccoli"? Instead, we turn to "comfort foods" like desserts. While "desserts" is "stressed" spelled backwards, these foods don't help our Limbo unwind. Whole plant-based foods are better for that, so follow the zebra's lead—sort of!

Rest well

When it comes to resting well, there are two lessons we can learn from zebras to help manage stress. The first is to get enough sleep, which was the topic of the previous chapter. Given there are no stories of zebras taking sleeping tablets, it is probably safe to say that they sleep well—even if not as long as humans. We should endeavour to do likewise to manage our stress levels.

But there is another aspect to the life of a zebra that probably helps them rest from stress. Zebras are in touch with the natural rhythms of life. On a macro level, they flow with yearly cycles— the seasons dictate their migratory behaviour. On a more micro level, they are in touch with the daily cycle—they watch the sun come up, peak and then go down.

When I was a university student, I worked as a lifeguard at a surf beach on Victoria's rugged coastline. Each day I would watch the sun come up and go down—like zebras do—but also the tide come in and go out. I discovered something profoundly connecting and calming about being in tune with these natural rhythms.

There is good evidence that humans also benefit from another rhythm of life—the weekly seven-day cycle, referred to as the *circaseptan* rhythm. Unlike the day, month and year, which are determined by the relative positions of the sun, moon and earth, there is no cosmological rationale for a seven-day cycle. But humans seem to respond well to a six-days-on, one-day-off cycle. Throughout history, governments have legislated different weekly cycles—France and Russia being notable examples—but we keep coming back to a seven-day, circaseptan cycle. It just seems to work best for us.

It has been known for many years that humans tend to display circaseptan rhythms in their health behaviours and outcomes. For example, heart rate, blood pressure and immune responses fluctuate during the week, leading to predictable weekly variations in heart attacks, strokes and the contraction of infectious diseases.[20]

In a fascinating study, researchers examined the death rates of Jews over a 10-year period and found a distinct circaseptan cycle,[21] in which death rates dipped on their Sabbath (Saturday), which is their "holy day". The premise behind Sabbath is to take an entire day off each week—the Jewish Sabbath extends from Friday sunset to Saturday sunset—from work and the busyness of life to celebrate, prioritise, balance and nurture the truly important things in life including health, happiness, relationships, connectedness and spirituality. The researchers titled the paper "Death rests a while" but the results of the study indicated

> The premise behind Sabbath is to take an entire day off each week . . . to celebrate, prioritise, balance and nurture the truly important things in life including health, happiness, relationships, connectedness and spirituality.

that it wasn't just the act of resting that had the death-defying effect. No dip in death rates were observed on other "holy days" that did not coincide with the weekly six-days-on, one-day-off cycle, despite these holy days being observed in much the same way as their Sabbath. Other studies have also shown health and wellbeing benefits of Sabbath adherence.[22]

Circaseptan effects on mood are also well documented.[23] In a massive study involving more than 250,000 people from the

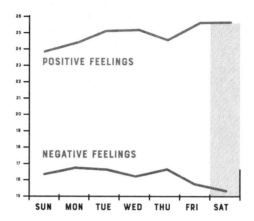

United States, the researchers found that people experienced the most positive feelings on Friday, Saturday and Sunday and the least negative feelings on Saturday and Sunday.[24] It seems that Saturday is the cheeriest day of the week!

Another study found that people's concern about their health, indicated by the number of recorded internet searches on related topics, fluctuates in a circaseptan manner.[25] As we saw earlier, one of the biggest causes of stress reported by people relates to their health and what they should be doing that they are not doing.[26] It seems that, once a week, people naturally take the pressure off themselves. It is like we are geared to need a stress-free day once a week.

There is a profound wisdom in the practice of Sabbath. In the 1960s and 1970s, economists forecast that, by the beginning of the 21st century, technological breakthroughs would allow us to work only a few hours a week and our main problem would be deciding what to do with all our leisure time.[27] Nothing could be further from the reality we are facing. We are working longer and longer hours, and it is taking its toll on every aspect of our lives. The principle of Sabbath offers an antidote to this ever-quickening pace of life, and the stress, anxiety, depression and burnout it leaves in its wake. It offers a rest we so desperately need, which can revitalise our physical, emotional, social and spiritual wellbeing.

The practice of Sabbath has always been an integral part of my life. I can't imagine life without it. I would go as far as saying that I don't know how people get by without it. Some people claim that they wouldn't get through all they need to do if they took one day out from work each week, but I have discovered that having a day off each week makes me more productive. It seems counter-intuitive, but time out rejuvenates and can provide clarity that we would not otherwise have.

To borrow an analogy from Steven Covey, author of *The 7 Habits of Highly Effective People*, it is like taking time to sharpen the saw.[28] Trying to cut through life with a blunt blade is unproductive. Taking time out to sharpen the saw can allow us to achieve more in less time. Even in my busiest periods of life, I have always prioritised one day out in seven. I don't check emails or even open my laptop—I endeavour to make it a "digital Sabbath"—and I don't feel guilty about it. It is my experience that practising Sabbath enhances my work, but more importantly, it enhances every aspect of my life—my relationships, my health and my happiness.

Putting it into action

1. LOL.

Laugh out loud! Seek out something that tickles your funny bone and causes you to laugh.

2. Sit in silence.

Take 15 minutes each day to sit in silence and be mindful.

3. Rest day.

Take a day off—no work. Don't even think about it! And make it a digital Sabbath by giving all your digital devices a rest too!

Recap

Life is stressful for many people. While it is sometimes difficult to turn down the heat, we can get better at opening the valves to relieve the pressure. In this regard, zebras can teach us a lot about using the SMILERS principle for relieving stress. Being physically active, practising mindfulness, laughing out loud and taking a Sabbath rest are all excellent strategies for dialling down our stress levels.

1. Australian Psychological Association (2015), "Stress and Wellbeing: How Australians are coping with life," <www.psychology.org.au/psychologyweek/survey/>.
2. American Psychological Association (2010), "Fact Sheet," <www.apa.org/practice/programs/workplace/phwp-fact-sheet.pdf>.
3. Australian Psychological Association, op cit.
4. ibid.
5. A Keller, K Litzelman, L E Wisk, T Maddox, E R Cheng, P D Creswell and W P Witt (2012), "Does the Perception that Stress Affects Health Matter? The Association with Health and Mortality," *Health Psychology*, 31(5), pages 677–84.

6. K McGonigal (2013), "How to make stress your friend," TEDGlobal2013, <www.ted.com/talks/kelly_mcgonigal_how_to_make_stress_your_friend>.

7. K Neirinckx, D Morton, W Herman and J Hinze (2015), "Don't stress me out! Anxiety, information processing and learning," *TEACH Journal,* 49(2), pages 42–50.

8. Australian Psychological Association, op cit.

9. R M Sapolsky (2004), *Why Zebras Don't Get Ulcers*, Henry Holt and Company.

10. E Kross, E Bruehlman-Senecal, J Park, A Burson, A Dougherty, H Shablack, R Brenmer, J Moser and O Arduk (2014), "Self-Talk as a Regulatory Mechanism: How You Do It Matters," *Journal of Personality and Social Psychology*, 106(2), pages 304–24.

11. Australian Psychological Association, op cit.

12. M Hamer, A Taylor and A Steptoe (2005), "The effect of acute aerobic exercise on stress related blood pressure responses: A systematic review and meta-analysis," *Biological Psychology*, 71(2), pages 183–90.

13. Harvard Medical School Special Health Report (2013), *Positive Psychology: Harnessing the power of happiness, mindfulness, and inner strength,* Harvard Health Publications; S L Keng, M J Smoski and C J Robins (2011), "Effects of Mindfulness on Psychological Health: A Review of Empirical Studies," *Clinical Psychology Review*, 31(6), pages 1041–56; J Sundquist, A Lilja, K Palmer, A A Memon, X Wang, L M Johansson and K Sundquist (2015), "Mindfulness group therapy in primary care patients with depression, anxiety and stress and adjustment disorders: Randomised controlled trial," *The British Journal of Psychiatry*, 206(2), pages 128–35.

14. B M Way, J D Creswell, N I Eisenberger and M D Lieberman (2010), "Dispositional Mindfulness and Depressive Symptomatology: Correlations with Limbic and Self-Referential Neural Activity during Rest," *Emotion,* 10(1), page 12–24.

15. S Scott (2015), "Why we laugh," TED2015, <www.ted.com/talks/sophie_scott_why_we_laugh>.

16. P McGhee (2010), *Humor: The lighter path to resilience and health,* Authorhouse Publishing.

17. Proverbs 17:22, KJV.

18. Scott, op cit.

19. B L Beezhold, C S Johnston and D R Daigle (2010), "Vegetarian diets are associated with healthy mood states: A cross-sectional study in Seventh Day Adventist adults," *Nutrition Journal*, 9:26, <www.nutritionj.com/content/9/1/26>.

20. J W Ayers, B M Althouse, M Johnson, M Dredze and J E Cohen (2014), "What's the Healthiest Day? Circaseptan (Weekly) Rhythms in Healthy

Considerations," *American Journal of Preventive Medicine*, 47(1), pages 73–6.

21. J Anson and O Anson (2001), "Death rests a while: Holy day and Sabbath effects on Jewish mortality in Israel," *Social Science and Medicine*, 52, pages 83–97.

22. D J Superville, K I Pargament and J W Lee (2014), "Sabbath Keeping and Its Relationships to Health and Well-Being: A Mediational Analysis," *The International Journal for the Psychology of Religion*, 24, pages 241–56.

23. G Cornelissen, D Watson, G Mitsutake, B Fiser, J Siegelova, J Dusek, I Vohlidalova, H Svacinova and F Halberg (2005), "Mapping of circaseptan and circadian changes in mood," *Scripta Medica (Brno)*, 78(2), page 89–98; A A Stone, S Schneider and J K Harter (2012), "Day-of-week mood patterns in the United States: On the existence of 'Blue Monday', 'Thank God it's Friday' and weekend effects," *The Journal of Positive Psychology*, 7(4), pages 306–14.

24. Stone, et al, op cit.

25. Ayers, et al, op cit.

26. Australian Psychological Association, op cit.

27. C Hamilton and R Denniss (2006), *Affulenza: When too much is never enough*, Allen & Unwin.

28. S Covey (1989), *The 7 Habits of Highly Effective People*, Free Press.

S·M·I·L·E·R·S

REST WELL: DESTRESS

Chapter 10
Giving is living

−Serve−

*I don't know what your destiny will be, but one thing I do know:
the only ones among you who will be really happy are those who
have sought and found how to serve.*—Albert Schweitzer

What a person plants, he will harvest.—The Message

We can learn a lot from children. I certainly have.

For example, did you know that the slot where you insert a CD in a car stereo is perfect for playing a game called "money box"? But be aware that, despite cramming as many coins as possible into the "money box," it still won't contain enough money to pay for the replacement stereo that will be necessary after the coins have destroyed the original "money box." This was a favourite game of my children, so much so that they played it twice!

But the best lessons you can learn from children are life lessons on how to live better. When my children were 10, nine and seven years old, my wife and I took them to Sydney to see the sights. In the early evening, we went for a walk through the heart of the bustling city. As we turned a corner, we were confronted by a homeless man who was on his knees, bent forward with his forehead touching the ground. His hands were poised above his head cradling a plastic cup, hoping for a handout.

The man looked dishevelled and untidy. His hair was matted and his clothes were torn. My immediate reaction was to veer to the opposite side of the footpath and I tugged at the hands of the two children I was leading. But, instead of following my lead, I felt a tug from my youngest, Caleb, in the opposite direction. To my alarm, I felt his hand slip from mine and, as I turned my head, I saw him move quickly *toward* the man. I caught him just as he bent down to reach out to the man, who was still kneeling with his head down.

Caleb looked up at me and said, "We have to help him, Daddy. Do you have some money?"

I hesitated for a moment. Ashamedly, my first thought was that, if I put money into the man's empty cup, I would simply be funding his next pack of cigarettes or bottle of alcohol. But in that moment, I also had an acute awareness that there was a greater lesson to be learned here. I reached into my pocket and handed Caleb some cash, which he placed in the man's cup.

That day, Caleb was the teacher—and I was the student.

Throughout this book, we have been learning about our Limbo, its sources of input and how to put it in a better place. In the previous chapters, we have seen how our Limbo is electrically wired and chemically charged. I hope you now have a good arsenal of strategies you can use to help you live more emotionally up and less down, and that you understand why and how these strategies work. But the anatomy lesson concludes here.

I can't illustrate using nerve pathways or detail the action of hormones to explain how this final strategy makes us happier and more emotionally well. But in a profound and powerful way, it does. From first-hand experience and the testimony of hundreds of people I have interviewed, the pursuit of deep emotional richness is tragically deficient if this final ingredient is absent. Science says so too.

Service To Others Really Matters

I was once dragged along on a week-long community service trip called STORM Co—meaning Service To Others Really Matters. It was organised by my wife for a group of 20 or so local high school students. It wasn't that I was opposed to the idea of community service, but I say "dragged along" because my life was just too hectic. At the time I was building a house, while completing a PhD degree—I was a busy man! But when they couldn't find a bus driver, I reluctantly agreed. In my mind, I gave up a week of "productivity" to do community service in a country town in rural Australia.

The experience was transformational. Since then, I have willingly—even enthusiastically—been back for several more week-long stints. Why? Each time I return home feeling emotionally energised. I have learned that, in the words of Abraham Lincoln, "When I do good, I feel good."

Scientists from several fields are converging on the fact that we humans seem to be wired to look out for others. In a fascinating article titled "The Samaritan Paradox"—published in *Scientific America Mind*—the authors concluded, "Our species is apparently the only one with a genetic makeup that promotes selflessness and true altruistic behaviour."[1] Something deep within us seems to embrace the paradox that, through giving, we receive. Through service, our spirits are lifted. It is good to be good.

Many studies testify to this. For example, studies show that

volunteering time to a worthwhile cause increases wellbeing, health and possibly even life span.[2] A large study in the United States indicated that volunteering once per week increased peoples' chances of being "very happy" with their lives by the same amount as moving from a personal income bracket of less than $20,000 per year, which is pretty much below the poverty line, to more than $75,000 per year.[3] Put another way, volunteering once per week can offer the same emotional lift as tripling our income!

In the same vein, service-oriented lawyers report higher levels of happiness than money-oriented lawyers, despite earning a much lower income.[4] Similarly, in other workplace environments, having a "service mentality" has been shown to be a more important motivator than increasing wages.[5] It seems that service beats money. But, in case you are thinking that money can't buy happiness, this is not entirely true. In a study in which people were given money to spend—they had no problems finding subjects for this study!—researchers found that spending money did cause a long-term spike in happiness, but only among those participants who were instructed to spend the money on someone else.[6]

Researchers from the University of North Carolina have even found that having an altruistic orientation up-regulates important genes involved in boosting our immune system.[7] What was interesting in the study is that they compared people who reported two different kinds of wellbeing. "Hedonic wellbeing" is characterised by having lots of positive psychological experiences, typically through self-gratification. In contrast, "eudaimonic wellbeing" results from striving for meaning and a noble purpose, often with a spirit of service. The researchers found that only people with high levels of "eudaimonic wellbeing" had boosted immune systems.

> *Serving changes the direction of our focus from inward to outward. It gets us outside our self, and this seems to help our Limbo.*

There is certainly something about getting outside ourselves that does us good. When we get emotionally down, there is a tendency to become more introspective and to *internalise* or *personalise*. We tend to focus more on ourselves, our concerns and worries, and they can become all encompassing. At its extreme, severely depressed people have been described as having "their minds turned agonisingly inward."[8]

Serving changes the direction of our focus from inward to outward. It gets us outside our self, and this seems to help our Limbo. Perhaps as we see the plight of others, we realise that ours might not be so bad after all, so we become better at *looking to the positive*. Perhaps by serving others, we create new social bonds, so become *immersed in an uplifting social environment*.

Perhaps in the act of serving, we are forced to *speak positively* or even *move dynamically*. Whatever the reason, serving lifts our Limbo and lifts us.

The story is told of a certain beloved priest who would often leave the village in the morning and venture into the surrounding countryside, returning home in the evening. The villagers puzzled over where he went, so one day they asked a young man to follow the priest at a distance. The young man observed the priest walk into the forest, disrobe and dress as a peasant, then spend the day gathering firewood for the widows who lived outside the village.

"So where does our beloved priest go?" the villagers asked the young man on his return. "Does he ascend to heaven?"

The young man replied, "Yes, perhaps even higher."

In considering all the studies that have been done on how to boost emotional wellbeing, former president of the American Psychological Association and widely regarded as the father of the "positive psychology movement," Martin Seligman concluded, "We scientists have found that doing a kindness produces the single most reliable increase in wellbeing (happiness) of any exercise we have tested."[9]

The takeaway message is that approaching life with an attitude of service is not only honourable, it is one of the best things we can do for ourselves. Service has even been described as "enlightened self-interest"—as compared to "self-sacrifice"—because the rewards that come from it do the doer such good.[10] The "helper's high" is a real and enduring buzz.[11]

I should point out that I am not encouraging you to be altruistic just so that you benefit. By definition, service that is self-seeking is not service at all. But feeling good is an undeniable consequence of serving, if you serve in the right way.

How to serve smart

In case you are getting nervous about what "serving" might mean for you and what you might be asked to give up, be encouraged to know that service doesn't mean having to sell all our possessions, giving the money to the poor and moving to Calcutta. It doesn't need to be grand scale to make a real difference. Even small "Random Acts of Kindness" (RAK) can give us an emotional lift.

We can be intentional and strategic with RAKs, such as paying the toll for the person in the car behind us or mowing an elderly lady's lawn. Or we can just be on the look-out for opportunities that present during the day. For some great and simple ideas on how to become a "RAKtivist," visit the Random Acts of Kindness website: <www.randomactsofkindness.org>.

> *Never underestimate the difference you might make in the world—at least someone's world—by a simple act of kindness.*

Never underestimate the difference you might make in the world—at least someone's world—by a simple act of kindness. The story is told of a boy walking along the beach where thousands of starfish had been washed ashore, facing a certain death. As he walked, he picked up one starfish at a time, throwing them back into the sea.

Amused by his futile efforts, a passerby called out, "Don't bother doing that, son. There are thousands of them, so it makes no difference."

The boy looked down at the starfish in his hand and called back, "It makes a difference to this one!"—and he threw it back into the sea.

155

We don't have to be Mother Teresa or Ghandi to make a difference. Even small random acts of kindness or a five-minute favour can add large value to the lives of others.

Of course, we can take service more seriously if we choose. As with most things in life, the more we give, the more we will likely get. There is a growing movement known as the "half-timers." Half-timers are those people who have been financially successful but, on reaching their middle years, realise they feel unfulfilled. Recognising a desire to move from success to significance, these individuals endeavour to make the second half of their lives really count through service—and some of them do remarkable things.

Like Ken Yeung, who describes himself as a "tea guy" who just so happens to also be passionate about orphans.[12] Ken has been tremendously successful in the tea industry, but in the second half of his life has redirected much of his wealth into caring for orphans in China, especially those who are physically and mentally disabled. Ken carries around with him an album containing photos of 100 children from the orphanage he funds. It is a record of his proudest achievements and greatest joy.

In many ways, it is "more blessed to give than receive." But, while the evidence for the benefits of service is overwhelming, there are also pitfalls to be avoided.[13] It is important that we learn how to *serve smart*.

1. Serve sincerely.

One of my favourite quotes to live by reads as follows: "Make a careful exploration of who you are and the work you have been given, and then sink yourself into that. Don't be impressed with yourself. Don't compare yourself to others. Each of you must take responsibility for doing the creative best you can with your own life."[14] I love this quote for many reasons and I have it on my office door, so all visitors can benefit from its wisdom.

First, I love that it says that we all have a "work" to do. We all have a contribution to make. You have a part to play. I believe that. And it is not so much what we do, but the spirit with which we do it that counts. So have you discovered the work you have been given to do?

Second, this quote identifies the biggest enemy to us making our unique contribution—comparing our self to others. Our strengths and skills are for service, not status. The problem with comparing our self to others is that we are likely to come to one of two conclusions: We are better or worse than them. Either one will disable our personal effectiveness. When we decide we are not as good as someone else, we begin to question our contribution and become distracted. Conversely, when we conclude that we are better than others and become impressed with our self, we set our self up for failure, because pride goes before a fall.

> *It is not so much what we do, but the spirit with which we do it that counts.*

I have learned these lessons the hard way. Many years ago, when I started to develop a professional speaking business, I wanted to become my very best, so I would sit in on presentations by other speakers as often as I could to see what I could learn—and assess how I was going.

If the speaker I heard was very good, I would often come away disheartened and despondent, feeling like I should give up. I would question: *If I can't do it as well as them, why should I bother?*

But things were no better on the occasions that I came away

from listening to a speaker whom I considered not very good. It made me feel proud. As a consequence, I would become complacent and it would invariably lead to me not doing my best and hence my presentations not being as well received.

I have learned that, as my favourite quote concludes, all we need to concern ourselves with is doing the creative best we can with our own lives. Keep your eyes fixed on *your* authentic contribution. Yes, learn from others and let them help you be your best, but don't make it a competition that can lead to discouragement or pride. As the saying goes, "Don't try to be anyone else, they are already taken." Serve sincerely.

In the words of Dr Seuss, "Today you are you, that is truer than true. There is no-one alive who is you-er than you!" So concentrate on the work *you* have been given to do, and do it to the very best of *your* ability.

2. Serve with your signature strengths.

As we travelled home in the bus from my first STORM Co experience, I made an interesting observation. I asked those on the trip what had given them the biggest "buzz" and they all responded differently.

For some, the highlight was visiting the residents at the local retirement village. For others, it was running a "kids' club" for the children of the town. Others enjoyed painting fences at the community centre or helping to repair a water leak and tidy the garden at an elderly couple's home. Liaising with some local shop owners to organise their support for a community project energised another individual on the team. The point is that we are all different, and we are all meant to serve differently. I have come to understand that our greatest highs come from sharing our greatest gifts.

Much has been written and researched about "signature strengths." One thing is certain: We are all different in our profile of strengths. Researchers have identified 24 signature strengths that grow out of six virtues. To discover your signature strengths, take the signature strengths test at <www.viacharacter.org/survey/>.

An increasing number of studies are showing that intentionally using our "signature strengths" is associated with higher levels of happiness and less depression.[15] One study found that how we use our signature strengths on one day affects our mood the next.[16]

"Use your signature strengths in a new way" is now some of the most common advice in positive psychology for increasing people's long-term happiness.[17] In one experiment, participants are asked to identify their top five signature strengths, then to use one of those strengths in a new and different way every day for a week. For example, someone who has "bravery" as one of their signature strengths might intentionally do or plan something adventurous. Someone for

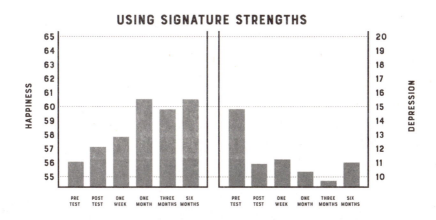

USING SIGNATURE STRENGTHS

whom "love of learning" is a top signature strength might do an internet search on a topic they are completely unfamiliar with to discover something new.

If people make a habit of intentionally using their signature strengths in a new way, it has been found to increase their happiness for years.[18] However, the key is to *use* our signature strengths, not just *identify* them.

In one study, individuals were asked to participate in one of three experiments. The first involved them *identifying* their signature strengths. The second involved *using* their signature strengths. The third experiment was called "you at your best" and involved them reflecting on a time when they were at their best and what strengths they displayed at the time. Only the people in the second group—those who *used* their signature strengths—reported an increase in happiness and a decrease in depressive symptoms, and the effect lasted for six months after the experiment.[19]

The other two groups experienced no such benefits. In fact, the "you at your best" group reported feeling more depressed, probably because the thought of how they used to be got them down! The lesson is that we must take action on our signature strengths if they are to benefit us. As Aristotle noted, "Happiness is the consequence of a deed."

But I would like to take this challenge a step further. As we have stated, our strengths and skill are for service, not status. While using our signature strengths can elevate us, using our signature strengths *for good* can lift us higher. As have many others, I have come to discover that the sweet spot in life is where what we love, what we are good at and what serves the world all intersect.

We will be most emotionally uplifted if we use our signature

strengths for service. We all have a unique set of talents and abilities. As suggested in the earlier quotation, "make a careful exploration of who you are" to discover them, then use them for good.

3. Serve sustainably.

The third consideration for *serving smart* relates to sustainability. While it is uplifting to serve, if we don't balance giving with receiving, we can experience burnout. Take the analogy of a watercourse. If a watercourse only receives but never gives, if water only flows in but not out, it eventually stagnates and putrefies, like the Dead Sea. This is the fate of people who consume but don't contribute. On the other hand, if a watercourse gives in excess of what it receives, it runs dry. We can run dry and suffer burnout if we don't receive. To serve smart, we need to balance the flow of giving and receiving.

Adam Grant is an organisational psychologist who has found this also true in companies. He compared the performance of "givers" and "takers" in the workplace and found some surprising results. It turns out that "givers" perform both better and worse than "takers". Those who give, give and give some more tend to burn out and perform the worst, but "successful givers"—those who recognise that it is OK, even necessary, to be receivers too—perform best.[20]

If you are someone who has a tendency to give and give but then find yourself running dry, you need to hear this message: You can't pour from an empty cup. It is good that you care and your heart for service is admirable, but you must learn to do it in a sustainable manner. Running dry is not good for anyone in the long term. It's not selfish to be filled—it's sustainable! Like a watercourse needs in-pouring from an outside source, so do you.

Practicing all the strategies we have been learning through this book can also help—speaking positively, taking time to be active, getting outside, spending time with friends, taking time out to rest—are all great ways to fill our cup. Then we can give again.

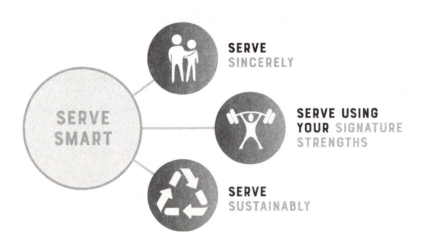

Reap what we sow

We have been learning about and exploring strategies for getting our Limbo—our Home of Happy—into a better place, so we can live more. It is my genuine desire that this has worked for you, that you are authentically happier for the experience and have the skills to be more emotionally resilient. But of all the strategies and exercises we have explored, I have come to believe that this last one—serving—has the potential to bring the greatest joy. I have observed that there is a universal law that governs our emotional life. It simply states that we *reap what we sow*.

As Martin Seligman says, if you want to be happy "do something to make someone else happy!"[21] If we purposefully and intentionally seek to lift others—to make them happier—we will rise with them. This is the heartbeat of service—to lift others—and as the old saying goes, "I'll lift thee, and you'll lift me, and we'll rise together."

Of course, there is a warning that comes with the truth that we reap what we sow. If we purposefully and intentionally seek to drag others down, we will go down with them as well. Throughout history, we can find examples of people who went through their life robbing others of their money, then died with lots of money—not that it did them much good. We can also find examples of people who went through their life robbing others of their power, then died with lots of power—not that it did them much good. But I cannot find one example of a sane person who went through their life robbing others of their happiness, then died happy themself. When it comes to happiness, the law of reaping what we sow is always returned to us in this lifetime.

So I encourage you to test and see. Serve smart. I am confident you will discover that it is good to do good. Service can lead to something greater than a "pleasant" life; it is a pathway to a "meaningful" life.[22] As Ghandi said, "The best way to find yourself is to lose yourself in the service of others."

Putting it into action

1. Become a RAKtivist.

Make a habit of doing Random Acts of Kindness. Take notice of its effect on you—the giver—as well as the receiver. You can either pre-plan it or just be on the lookout to show kindness when the opportunity arises!

2. Use your signature strengths in a new way for good.

Make a careful exploration of who you are by identifying your signature strengths. What comes easily to you? What are you passionate about? What strengths do others see in you? Discover what they are and get creative about ways you can activate them for good, then do it!

Recap

To give is to truly live. Scientific studies and personal experiences confirm that humans have an inbuilt desire to contribute and serve, and doing so is emotionally uplifting. By serving smart—with sincerity, using our signature strengths, and sustainably—we can discover not only a happier life, but a more meaningful one as well. We can live more!

1. E Fehr and S Renninger (2004), "The Samaritan Paradox: If we live in a dog-eat-dog world, then why are we frequently so good to each other?" *Scientific American Mind*, 14(5), pages 15–21.

2. S G Post (2005), "Altruism, Happiness, and Health: It's Good to Be Good," *International Journal of Behavioral Medicine*, 12(2), pages 66–77.

3. F Borgonovi (2008), "Doing well by doing good: The relationship between formal volunteering and self-reported health and happiness," *Social Science & Medicine*, 66, pages 2321–34.

4. K M Sheldon and L S Krieger (2014), "Service job lawyers are happier than money job lawyers, despite their lower income," *The Journal of Positive Psychology*, 9(3), pages 219–26.

5. J Taylor and R Taylor (2011), "Working Hard for More Money or Working Hard to Make a Difference? Efficiency Wages, Public Service Motivation, and Effort," *Review of Public Personnel Administration*, 31, page 67.

6. E W Dunn, L A Aknin and M I Norton (2008), "Spending money on others promotes happiness," *SCIENCE*, 319, pages 1687–88.

7. B L Fredrickson, K M Grewen, K A Coffey, S B Algoe, A M Firestine, J M G Arevalo, J Ma and S W Cole (2013), "A functional genomic perspective on human well-being," *Proceedings of the National Academy of Sciences*, 110(33), pages 13684–9.

8. W Styron (1992), *Darkness Visible: A memoir of madness*, Vintage, page 47.

9. M Seligman (2011), *Flourish*, Random House, page 20.

10. R Walsh (1999), *Essential Spirituality: The seven central practices*, Wiley.

11. S G Post, L G Underwood, J P Schloss and W B Hurlbut (2002), *Altruism and Altruistic Love: Science, philosophy and religion in dialogue*, Oxford University Press.

12. Half-time Institute, "Kenneth Yeung: Pictures Saving Orphans," <halftimeinstitute.org/stories/kenneth-yeung-pictures-saving-orphans/>.

13. R Walsh (2011), "Lifestyle and Mental Health," *American Psychologist*, 66(7), pages 579–92.

14. Galatians 6:4, 5, *The Message*.

15. R T Proyer, F Gander, S Wellenzohn, and W Ruch (2015), "Strengths-based positive psychology interventions: A randomized placebo-controlled online trial on long-term effects for a signature strengths vs. a lesser strengths-intervention," *Frontiers in Psychology*, 6, page 456; M E Seligman, T A Steen, N Park and C Peterson (2005), "Positive Psychology Progress. Empirical Validation of Interventions," *American Psychologist*, 60(5), pages 410–21.

16. S Lavy, H Littman-Ovadia, and Y Bareli (2014), "Strengths deployment as a mood-repair mechanism: Evidence from a diary study with a relationship exercise group," *Journal of Positive Psychology*, 9(6), pages 547–58.

17. R T Proyer, F Gander, S Wellenzohn and W Ruch (2014), "Positive psychology interventions in people aged 50–79 years: Long-term effects of placebo-controlled online interventions on well-being and depression," *Aging & Mental Health*, 18(8), pages 997–1005; Seligman, et al (2005), op cit.

18. R T Proyer, S Wellenzohn, F Gander, W Ruch (2014), "Toward a better understanding of what makes positive psychology interventions work: Predicting happiness and depression from the person × intervention fit in a follow-up after 3.5 years," *Applied Psychology: Health and Well-Being*, 7(1), pages 108–28.

19. M E Seligman, et al (2005), op cit.

20. Adam Grant, "Are you a giver or a taker?" TED, <www.ted.com/talks/adam_grant_are_you_a_giver_or_a_taker#t-353550>.

21. M Seligman (2002), *Authentic Happiness*, Random House.

22. R F Baumeister, K D Vohs, J L Aaker and E N Garbinsky (2015), "Some key differences between a happy life and a meaningful life," *Journal of Positive Psychology*, 8(6), pages 505–16.

S·M·I·L·E·R·S

SERVE

Chapter 11

What it takes to flourish

We all live with the objective of being happy; our lives are all different and yet the same.—Anne Frank

What's the use of happiness? It can't buy you money!—Henry Youngman

A long time back—when I was a college student—I opened a bank account to save for a new (used) car. After almost a year, I had saved $2000 and still had a way to go, so a friend gave me a saving tip. He suggested that, instead of putting the money in a bank account where it generated a measly interest rate, I should invest in the stock market and purchase shares in the bank. It sounded risky to me, but he assured me it was very safe and a great idea.

Following his advice, I nervously opened a trading account, then calculated how many shares I could purchase with my $2000. After checking my calculations, then checking them again—and again—I pressed "Buy." It was nerve-racking but also quite exhilarating to think that I now had a "portfolio"! Just four days later, my exhilaration faded when I learned that the stock market had taken a dive.

To make matters worse, I received a letter confirming my

purchase that made my heart sink. Instead of purchasing 50 shares, I had accidently purchased 500 shares! At first I couldn't believe it was possible—after all, I didn't have enough money in my account to purchase that many shares. So I contacted the bank only to learn that it had generously allowed me to overdraw on my account by $24,000! Ahhh! Feeling nauseous, I looked to see how much of a dive my shares had taken over the previous few days.

Imagine my relief when I saw that while the stock market had fallen overall, my particular shares had gone up! As quickly as I could, I hit the "Sell" button and, to cut a long story short, I made almost $2000. I had doubled my money—in four days, by accident, with money I didn't have! Suddenly, I was riding high.

Up, down, up, down—the circumstances of our life can be like that. One of the intentions of this book is to equip you with strategies to be more emotionally resilient, so that how you feel isn't a slave to the ups and downs of life. We might not be able to control the direction the wind blows us in, but we can decide how we set our sails and hence the direction we go.

I genuinely hope that you will use the strategies presented in this book to help put you on a more even keel. I use them all the time. If I need a pick-me-up, I look down the SMILERS list and can usually find one—or more—that can help fix how I feel. I really hope you can use the SMILERS approach in the same way, so you can be more emotionally resilient and "up" more of the time.

But if you want to truly *flourish* in life, the science says you need more than to just feel good. Five things are necessary.

What does it take to flourish?

In 1997, Dr Martin Seligman was voted the president of the American Psychological Association and he decided to invest his energies and influence into a new field of psychology. Dr Seligman noted that traditionally psychology had concerned itself only with the negative—devoting all its attention toward remedying dysfunctional psychological states—so he determined instead to investigate and promote what he referred to as *positive psychology*.[1]

Since that time, the field of positive psychology has exploded, and hundreds of experiments have been conducted, observations made and articles published. The intent of positive psychology is to scientifically understand and promote thriving individuals, families and communities in order to make "normal" lives more fulfilling.[2]

> *The intent of positive psychology is to scientifically understand and promote thriving individuals, families and communities in order to make "normal" lives more fulfilling.*

Initially the positive psychology literature focused on *happiness*—what causes it, how to achieve it, and what it is good for. However, while happiness is a worthy pursuit, the field of positive psychology has noted that it takes more than just smiles and giggles to thrive in life. More recently, Dr Seligman has suggested that there is a higher ideal: To *flourish*.[3]

"Flourish" is a more comprehensive measure of what it takes to live well and it encapsulates five domains that he sums up by the acronym PERMA. Personally, I prefer that the letters in PERMA be rearranged as PEARM. And Dr Seligman has indicated to me in personal communication that he feels the order is arbitrary, so I have taken the liberty to do it!

So let's consider what it takes to live a life that flourishes.

1. Positive Emotion

The primary focus of this book has been to share strategies for boosting our experience of positive emotions. There is no doubt that when we feel good, life is more enjoyable. So positive emotions are foundational to a life that flourishes.

In his earlier work, Dr Seligman used the term "pleasure" as compared to "positive emotion" and it is good that he updated it, because positive emotion represents much more than just cheap thrills. In fact, trying to build our wellbeing and happiness on pleasure alone is problematic. It is impossible to be constantly pleased. Pleasure is never permanent and laughter is never limitless. Even the funniest jokes, which had us rolling on the floor laughing the first time we heard them, lose their impact after a few tellings. And when pleasure is over, it's over. An episode of uncontrollable laughter will not satisfy us for weeks—or even days.

To achieve a flourishing life through the pursuit of pleasure, we would need to constantly busy ourselves seeking it. For these reasons, John D Rockefeller once said, "I can think of nothing less pleasurable than a life devoted to pleasure." It is interesting that several studies have found that pleasure does not correlate well with people's rating of their overall wellbeing.[4]

On the other hand, positive emotion includes not only excitement and ecstasy, but also other states such as happiness, contentedness and peace. People who experience more positive emotion are more satisfied with their life and report higher levels of flourishing[5] and I hope, through this book, you have discovered proven and practical paths to positive emotion!

2. Engagement

Have you ever been so completely engrossed in an activity that when you looked up some time later you were surprised by how much time had passed?

A pioneering researcher in the field of positive psychology, Dr Mihaly Csikszentmihalyi has intensively studied an experience he refers to as "flow."[6] Flow is a state of heightened focus and enjoyment that occurs in activities such as art, play and even work!

Not surprisingly, individuals who report high levels of flow in their daily activities, leading to *engagement*, also report higher levels of life satisfaction and flourishing.

> *It is ideal to find employment that engages us, because we spend so much of our time at work.*

Given that "engagement" is a powerful contributor to our ability to flourish, it is ideal to find employment that engages us, because we spend so much of our time at work. The story is told of a man who went to inspect a quarry where men were at work cleaving large bricks. He approached a worker and asked, "What are you doing?"

The worker looked up, agitated by the question, and replied, "What does it look like I'm doing? You've got eyes. Can't you see I am labouring away under this stinking hot sun making these stupid bricks!"

The visitor moved to a second worker and asked the same question, to which came the reply, "Oh, we are making these bricks and getting them smooth. It pays the bills. One day I might get promoted and move into the office."

Finally, the man noticed a worker who seemed highly engaged in what he was doing, meticulously smoothing the bricks. The man approached him and asked, "What are you doing?"

With enthusiasm, the worker looked up and said, "We are building a grand cathedral!"

The first worker had a job, the second a career, but the third a calling. Callings are the most engaging. So I hope you can discover yours.

Unfortunately, a Gallup poll found that, when workers were asked the question, "Do you like what you do each day?" only about 20 per cent replied with a strong "Yes." If we are not engaged in our work, it makes it even more critical that we engage in regular play. By definition, play refers to activities done for the sheer enjoyment of it—no extrinsic reward required! Adults tend to lose the capacity to play, which is tragic. Engaging in play is considered a sign of intelligence in the animal kingdom—monkeys play, dogs play, dolphins play, amoebas don't! So it is ironic that, while children are the masters of play, adults seem to lose the ability. We need to reclaim it.

Engagement is the second step on the path to flourishing. However, even individuals who enjoy much positive emotion and are regularly in a state of flow can still find something lacking in their life. To completely flourish, more is required.

3. Accomplishment

Are you the kind of person who judges whether a day has been good or bad according to how many items on your "To do" list you were able to tick off? If you are that kind of person, you will concur that there is something very rewarding about achieving something that you have set your mind to. Unfortunately, if you are that kind of person, you probably also have a tendency to overestimate what you are capable of achieving in any given day, so invariably feel dissatisfied with how few of the items on your list you crossed off!

Dr Seligman suggests that a sense of accomplishment, achievement, success or mastery helps people flourish. Accomplishment can be achieved in many domains including sport, business or education. Sometimes it is measured through agreed standards, such as competitions, awards or performing at a particular level. At an individual level, accomplishment can be defined in terms of achieving a desired state or attaining a goal.[7]

Accomplishment can enrich our lives independently of positive emotion or engagement. Indeed, there are many tasks that might not engage us or fill us with positive emotions while we perform them, yet on completion we discover a deep satisfaction that adds value to our life and even motivates us to do it again. Athletes often talk about how painful an event was and how the last stage of the race felt like it would never end—clearly they weren't enjoying positive emotions or in a state of flow at the time—but after the event, they start planning their next one.

> *Accomplishment can enrich our lives independently of positive emotion or engagement.*

Undoubtedly, the achievement of worthwhile pursuits can add value to our lives. However, as with positive emotion and engagement, it is not without its pitfalls. Most notably, accomplishment can be addictive and cause us to constantly chase bigger and better conquests. In itself that is not bad, except when it unbalances our life and sabotages other vitally important ingredients of a life that flourishes, such as the "R" in PEARM that we will explore next.

As a person who has suffered from accomplishment addiction, let me share one of the most valuable life lessons I learned nearly 20 years ago. It is easy to fall into the trap of thinking that accomplishment is the path to a *successful* life. After all, we tend to look to people who have earned a number of degrees, amassed great wealth or become famous and label them a "success." Ironically, I know many people who have achieved such things and their life isn't flourishing. In many cases, the pursuit of accomplishment has contributed to their unhappiness.

Some time back I realised that the most meaningful successes I had enjoyed in my life—the ones that really did add to my life—were not those that had come about by me doggedly going after them. Instead, they had arisen from opportunities that had presented themselves in ways that I could not have orchestrated. Since that time, I have adopted the wisdom of Mother Theresa who advised that "We are not called to be successful; we are called to be faithful."

Today, I try to be courageous enough to step through the doors of opportunity that open before me if I feel that my skills can be of service—that is what being faithful means to me. Whether they lead to "success" as measured by someone else's metric is not my concern. I am just called to do the best I can with what I have. This approach to life has liberated me and I have discovered the words of Victor Frankl to be true: "Success, like happiness, cannot be pursued; it must ensue . . . as the unintended side effect of one's personal dedication to a cause greater than oneself."[8]

4. Relationships

In Chapter 5, we explored the value of positive relationships for boosting wellbeing. As we learned, *together feels better* and we are designed to thrive in community. It has been concluded, "The belief that one is cared for, loved, esteemed and valued has been recognised as one of the most (if not the most) influential determinants of wellbeing for people of all ages and cultures."[9] Humans are relational creatures and our deepest levels of wellbeing seem to be realised by loving and being loved. We seek connectedness and that connectedness helps us to flourish.

5. Meaning

Having a sense of meaning is a fundamental need of humans. It's difficult, perhaps impossible, to live a truly flourishing life without it. It could be considered the most important of all the ingredients. We can live a life filled with fun times, be engaged in our daily activities, achieve noteworthy accomplishments and have positive relationships, yet still in our quieter moments wonder what's the point of it all. On the flip side, having a sense of meaning can make us come alive and lift us, even when the P, E, A and R are not going well for us. It is for this reason that I prefer PEARM to PERMA—it saves the best for last!

To put this in context: the P in PEARM—Positive emotion—can lead us to a "pleasant life" and that's good. Add the E, A and R—Engagement, Accomplishment and Relationships—and we move to a "good life" and that's great. Add to this the M—Meaning—and we discover a "meaningful life" and that's amazing.

Dr Seligman defines meaning as having a "feeling of *belonging* to and *serving* something bigger than the self."[10] In the previous chapter, we considered the notion of *serving* and how this can lift us. But for me personally, the belief that I *belong* to something bigger than myself gives me a sense of meaning, purpose and self-worth that I couldn't find in any other way.

I am almost embarrassed to share this story because it shows my ignorance. When my middle child—Liji—was just a toddler, I would kiss him each evening as I tucked him in bed and I would say, "Daddy loves you," and each evening he would ask me "Why?"

It became something of a game, as each evening I would give him a different reason: "Because you are so good at climbing trees!" or "Because you are so clever." It was only after a month or so that it dawned on me how inadequate my responses were and I then knew how I must reply. That evening, as I kissed him goodnight and said, "Daddy loves you," he predictably came back with "Why?" Without hesitating, I said, "Because you are mine. And there is nothing you can do—good or bad—to change that."

I hold a worldview that says *you belong* to something greater than yourself and that this belonging makes you immeasurably valuable. Your life has meaning. For me, knowing this is an absolute game-changer that lifts every aspect of my life and enables me to truly flourish. I would love for you to discover it too.

Putting it into action

1. Go with the flow!

What do you love to do that really captivates your attention and causes time to fly by? Do more of it!

2. Go after a goal.

What is something that you would like to achieve, that would give you a sense of accomplishment once completed? Make plans to go after that goal by writing the goal down and then list the steps you would need to take to make the goal.

3. Discover meaning.

What would you need to do or accept to discover a greater sense of meaning in your life?

Recap

The science says that to live a full and flourishing life you need to: encounter positive emotions, be engaged in life, experience a sense of accomplishment, enjoy positive relationships, and have an underpinning sense of meaning. Which of these might you strengthen to live more? Do all five to thrive.

It is my genuine hope that what you have discovered in this book can lift you and help you to live more fully and abundantly—to flourish!

Live your best life.

Live more happy!

1. M Seligman (2002), *Authentic Happiness*, Free Press.

2. M Seligman and M Csikszentmihalyi (2000), "Positive Psychology: An Introduction," *American Psychologist*, 55(1), pages 5–14.

3. M Seligman (2011), *Flourish*, Simon & Schuster.

4. N Park, C Peterson and W Ruch (2009), "Orientations to happiness and life satisfaction in twenty-seven nations," *The Journal of Positive Psychology,* 4(4), pages 273–9; S M Schueller and M E P Seligman (2010), "Pursuit of pleasure, engagement, and meaning: Relationships to subjective and objective measures of well-being," *The Journal of Positive Psychology*, 5(4), pages 253–63.

5. E Diener and R Biswas-Diener (2008), *Happiness: Unlocking the mysteries of psychological wealth*, Wiley-Blackwell; Seligman (2011), op cit.

6. M Csikszentmihalyi (2013), *Flow: The Psychology of Happiness*, Ebury Digital.

7. M J C Forgeard, E Jayawickreme, M Kern and M E P Seligman (2011), "Doing the right thing: Measuring wellbeing for public policy," *International Journal of Wellbeing,* 1(1), pages 79–106.

8. V Frankl (1946), *Man's Search for Meaning*, Beacon Press.

9. H Reis and S Gable (2003), "Toward a positive psychology of relationships," in C Keyes and J Haidt (editors), *Flourishing: Positive psychology and the life well-lived*, American Psychological Association.

10. Seligman (2011), op cit.

S SPEAK POSITIVELY

M MOVE DYNAMICALLY

I IMMERSE IN AN UPLIFTING
PHYSICAL & SOCIAL ENVIRONMENT

L LOOK TO THE POSITIVE

E EAT NUTRITIOUSLY

R REST WELL: SLEEP / STRESS LESS

S SERVE

Dr Darren Morton is a Fellow of the Australasian Society of Lifestyle Medicine and Course Coordinator of Postgraduate Studies in Lifestyle Medicine at Avondale College of Higher Education in Cooranbong, New South Wales, Australia. He is a regular public and corporate speaker on topics of wellbeing and positive psychology, and is co-presenter of the Complete Health Improvement Program (CHIP), a lifestyle medicine program that operates in more than 10 countries. His research has been published in leading medical and scientific journals, and this is his third book.

For more on Live More Happy, Dr Darren Morton, his programs and other books, visit:

www.DrDarrenMorton.com

Bring *Live More Happy* to life by joining
The Lift Project: <www.theliftproject.global>.